The Heritage Book 1991

Edna McCann

Collier Macmillan Canada, Inc.

Collier Macmillan Canada, Inc.
1200 Eglinton Ave. East, Suite 200
Don Mills, Ontario   M3C 3N1

ISBN 02.953937.4

Printed and bound in Canada

Fifteenth Edition

"Robin" by Emily Dickinson is reprinted by permission of the Harvard College Library.

"White Fields" by James Stephens, from *An Inheritance of Poetry* © Riverside Press, Houghton Mifflin Co., 1948.

PICTURE CREDITS

Winter
Charlene Daley
Florence Gillespie
Charlene Daley
Rick Sirois
Patrick Gallagher
Charlene Daley
Charlene Daley

Spring
Florence Gillespie
Cathie Archbould
Charlene Daley
Nikki Abraham
Cathie Archbould
Nikki Abraham

Summer
Charlene Daley
Patrick Gallagher
Nikki Abraham
Charlene Daley
Cathie Archbould
Charlene Daley

Autumn
Charlene Daley
Cathie Archbould
Cathie Archbould
Charlene Daley
Cathie Archbould
Charlene Daley

Cover photo: Florence Gillespie
Cover design: Laffey Design

THIS is the fifteenth edition of *The Heritage Book*, a fact that rather amazes me! Isn't it astounding to reflect on how much our lives and our world have changed in what has seemed, to me, such a brief time? Many recent events have forever altered the way we see this Earth and our fellow humans; we have learned that we are more alike than we are different. Most importantly, we all want a better world for our children and our children's children. As citizens of the same small, fragile planet, we still have much to learn in order to attain this goal, but I am reassured by the commitment to family, faith, and community that I know many already share.

I am deeply grateful for the opportunity to have shared this little book with so many of you for fifteen years. I wish you much joy and laughter as you work toward your goals in 1991.

Edna McCann

January

E ACH day is an opportunity to start all over again, to cleanse our minds and hearts anew and to clarify our vision. And let us not clutter up today with the leavings of other days.

— *Oliver Wendell Holmes*

What an excellent thought with which to begin a new year. The old year is past, and we have 365 new days in a new year to live to the fullest.

Let us not "clutter up" this year with "the leavings" of other years.

WEDNESDAY — JANUARY 2

A FTER the hustle and bustle of the holiday season it's nice to spend a quiet day alone.

I spent this day in my chair in front of a warm fire and with many cups of hot tea and cocoa. It was especially pleasant because I had some excellent reading material. Many of the Christmas cards that I received had long "newsy" letters enclosed, but in the busy time before Christmas I didn't really have time to enjoy them. Today I was able to take the time to appreciate the news of children, grandchildren, their happy times, their accomplishments, and, in a few cases, their sorrows.

All of these lovely letters brought back wonderful memories of times that we had shared together.

So although I spent today by myself I was certainly not alone.

Memories make wonderful companions.

THURSDAY — JANUARY 3

T HE good thing about dreams is that if they don't come true you can always dream new ones.

THE HERITAGE BOOK

MY good friend Jake Frampton stopped by this evening and was easily persuaded to stay for the evening meal with Marg, Bruce and myself.

As my former readers know, Jake owns a small bookstore and he often brings us books or magazines that he knows will interest us. This evening was no exception.

My son-in-law, Bruce, has always been very interested in the field of aviation, and Jake brought several books for Bruce that outlined the history of flight, beginning as far back as the 1800s, when man first flew in hot-air balloons.

One of the books that Bruce quickly became engrossed in was *Men from Earth*, by astronaut Buzz Aldrin, one of the three men who journeyed to the moon on the Apollo 11 spacecraft in July, 1969.

I was interested to hear that even as he looked at the American flag, planted on the lunar surface on that earth-shaking July 20, his vision was of manned flights beyond the moon. He would like to see NASA step up manned exploration of the solar system. Perhaps his dreams will be realities some day soon.

SATURDAY — JANUARY 5

THE most successful salespeople, teachers, writers, politicians, and others who deal with people know this one simple fact: every person in the world is hungry — if not for food, then for recognition, companionship, a helping hand, understanding, love — the list is endless. Knowing this will help you in any walk of life. The one who satisfies the most hunger in others will always be the most successful — and the happiest.

SUNDAY — JANUARY 6

IN the Christian tradition, this is the day on which the Three Kings, the first Gentiles to acknowledge the wonder of God's gift, the Christ child, brought their gifts of love and adoration. In their humble action they proclaimed the universality of the Christ child.

"O God, who by the leading of a star didst manifest thy only-begotten Son to the Gentiles; Mercifully grant, that we, which know thee now by faith, may after this life have the fruition of thy glorious Godhead; through Jesus Christ our Lord. Amen."

— The Book of Common Prayer

THE HERITAGE BOOK

A NNOUNCED by all the trumpets of the sky
Arrives the snow, and, driving o'er the
fields,
Seems nowhere to alight; the whited air
Hides hills and woods, the river, and the
heaven,
And veils the farmhouse at the garden's end.

The sled and traveler stopped, the courier's
feet
Delayed, all friends shut out, the housemates
sit
Around the radiant fireplace, enclosed
In a tumultuous privacy of storm.
—*Ralph Waldo Emerson*

M OST of us who are grandparents have
secret hopes and ambitions for those
adorable young people who are our grandchildren. This little anecdote appealed to me very
much.

A grandmother was walking her daughter's
young children at the mall when a lady said to
her, "My, what adorable children. How old are
they?"

"The doctor is three," replied the proud
grandmother, "and the ambassador is five."

WEDNESDAY — JANUARY 9

IT isn't how much you know but what you get done that the world rewards and remembers.

—Alfred A. Montapert

THURSDAY — JANUARY 10

"INTUITION" is what a woman gives as the explanation when she doesn't want to tell a man that she's smarter than he is.

FRIDAY — JANUARY 11

MAKING marriage work is like operating a farm. You have to start all over again each morning.

THE HERITAGE BOOK

THIS was a wonderful, if exhausting, day. Marg, Bruce, and I joined Phyllis, Bill, and their twins Justin and Jenny for a day at the country home of my grandson Fred, his wife June, and their sons Mickey and Geoffrey.

It was a glorious day for a drive. The snow sparkled and the ice on the trees shone like diamonds. Jenny sat quietly, drinking in the scenery as we travelled, while Justin was non-stop questions and chatter.

When we arrived, Fred and June had a most enjoyable day planned for us.

The children spent the morning flying down the big hill on their sleds and saucers, then scampering back up to do it again.

We adults sat before a fire and had a wonderful visit, our first since Christmas. After a hearty lunch of hot chili, Fred hitched their horse to an old-fashioned sleigh and we had a lovely tour of the area.

What powerful memories were evoked! It didn't seem that long ago that I travelled with my father in our old cutter on Canada's east coast.

Time spent with the family is such a joy to me. I have many more pleasant memories to file.

THE HERITAGE BOOK

COME, Holy Spirit, wisdom and truth:
Strengthen us in the risk of faith.
Come Holy Spirit, come.
— *Book of Alternative Service*

THE house-dog on his paws outspread
Laid to the fire his drowsy head,
The cat's dark silhouette on the wall
A couchant tiger's seemed to fall;
And, for the winter's fireside meet,
The mug of cider simmered slow,
The apples sputtered in a row,
And close at hand the basket stood
With nuts from brown October's wood.
— *John Greenleaf Whittier*

TODAY is the birthday of Martin Luther King. Dr. King once wrote about a seventy-two-year-old woman who walked a long distance every day in support of a bus boycott. When asked why, she answered, "My feet is tired, but my soul is at rest." What a wonderful tribute to Dr. King's ideals.

THE HERITAGE BOOK

I SPENT just a short time outdoors today. I had planned a longer walk, but the wind seemed to chill me right to the bone, and I turned for home much sooner than usual.

Today's intensely cold weather reminded me of a story that my husband George and I followed with interest many years ago.

Back in 1934, forty-six-year-old American Richard E. Byrd spent four and one half months in isolation in the forbidding environment of the Ross Ice Barrier in the Antarctic.

The Rolling Advance Weather Base was set up to keep important weather records of the 4,500,000-square-mile Antarctic Continent. At that time it was a meteorological blank. Byrd proposed to combine this data with data collected at "Little America" on the coast to reveal atmospheric conditions in the hemisphere.

Admiral Byrd survived temperatures as low as -80°F, carbon monoxide poisoning (from a faulty stove pipe), long months of blackness, and the psychological effects of isolation.

His survival and reports of his work are a lasting testament to human courage and endurance.

THURSDAY — JANUARY 17

A LLAN Fromme, psychologist, has this to say about self-discovery:

One of the greatest advantages of our later years is that we no longer have to scream; we can talk. We don't have to run; we can walk. We have the time to examine the quality of life and to work for ourselves on its improvement. We need no longer feel driven by idols of the market place. We can do more of what we like, rather than what we were told we'd like. It's this period that offers the opportunity for self-rediscovery, and one of the refreshing things we learn all over again is the essential truth of the architectural adage, "Less is more."

FRIDAY — JANUARY 18

L EARNING without thought is labour lost; thought without learning is perilous.

— Confucius

THE HERITAGE BOOK

YESTERDAY'S mail brought a letter from my dear friend Mavis Tewbury. Several years ago Mavis took up the sport of cross-country skiing and she has enjoyed many pleasant winter holidays practising her recently acquired skills.

Her most recent trip was to Banff, in Canada's western province of Alberta. Although this area is more widely known for its downhill ski areas, the increased popularity of cross-country skiing has prompted resorts to establish trails for enthusiasts.

In her letter Mavis tells of well-groomed trails and magnificent scenery.

"It was almost more beautiful than you could imagine, Edna. We skied along wooded trails that were perfectly groomed for easy skiing. Each time that we emerged from the woods we had the majestic snow-covered Rocky Mountains to gaze upon. The sun shone over the top of the hills and suddenly the snow would turn a magnificent pink-gold. I think that I can truly understand the word 'breathtaking' now. Each of these trips reminds me of how pleased I am to have found this sport, even at my age!"

SUNDAY — JANUARY 20

ALMIGHTY God, You have made us for yourself; our hearts are restless until they find their rest in you. May we find praise in your service, and in the world to come, see you face to face.

Amen.
— *A prayer of St. Augustine*

MONDAY — JANUARY 21

TWO things worry people most these days: one, that things may never get back to normal; and the other, that they have already.

TUESDAY — JANUARY 22

I ENJOYED comedian Bob Hope's comment on birthdays.
"You know you're getting old when the candles cost more than the cake."

THE HERITAGE BOOK

THOSE of you who have pets and know of the strong attachments that many people form with their animals will appreciate the findings of an American medical research team, who found that both long- and short-term hospital patients seemed to heal more quickly when they spent time with animals.

Because of this, many nursing homes and hospitals are allowing "visiting privileges" to pets, and some chronic care units have even "adopted" animals, allowing them to visit freely with patients.

Often their presence can have a dramatic effect. Ethel, an elderly lady in a nursing home, had spoken to no one since the death of her husband many months before. Family members and staff had tried in vain to bring her out of her self-imposed silence.

One day, tiny Fluffy launched her feline body onto Ethel's bed, where she snuggled on the blanket, looking up into her eyes. Ethel's eyes lit up and she began to croon "cute kitty, sweet kitty" — not a surprise to pet lovers.

THE HERITAGE BOOK

THE rung of a ladder was never meant to rest upon but only to hold a man's foot long enough to enable him to put the other somewhat higher.

— *Thomas Henry Huxley*

THROUGH this toilsome world, alas!
Once and only once I pass;
If a kindness I may show,
If a good deed I may do
To a suffering fellow man,
Let me do it while I can.
No delay, for it is plain
I shall not pass this way again.

SATURDAY — JANUARY 26

CHARLES Darwin wrote some interesting lines on music and poetry:

"If I had my life to live over again, I would have made a rule to read some poetry and listen to some music at least once a week; for perhaps the parts of my brain now atrophied would thus have kept active through use.

The loss of these tastes is a loss of happiness, and may possibly be injurious to the intellect, and more probably the moral character, by enfeebling the emotional part of our nature."

SUNDAY — JANUARY 27

AND as he was going along by the sea of Galilee, He saw Simon and Andrew, the brother of Simon, casting a net in the sea; for they were fishermen.

And Jesus said to them, "Follow Me, and I will make you fishers of men."

And they immediately left the nets and followed Him.

— *Mark 1:16-18*

THE HERITAGE BOOK

My sister Sarah and I had a wonderful visit by telephone this weekend. Sarah lives on Canada's east coast, so our face-to-face visits are infrequent. We do keep in touch by letter or phone very regularly, however.

This week Sarah called to tell me how much she was enjoying her new job. She is now the person responsible for the "Meals on Wheels" program in her area. This service of providing meals to the elderly and shut-ins is a very important part of community life, so Sarah's responsibility is enormous.

The community made a clever choice; from the time that she was a young girl, Sarah has been a tremendous organizer. She organized bazaars at the church, led the youth organization and fund-raising drives, and so on. She always put her heart and soul into all of these activities, a true giver of herself.

I hope "Meals on Wheels" realize how lucky they are to have someone as dedicated as my sister will be.

Man does not live by words alone, despite the fact that he sometimes has to eat them.

—*Adlai Stevenson*

THE HERITAGE BOOK

M AN cannot discover new oceans unless he has the courage to lose sight of the shore.
— *André Gide*

A GOOD friend of mine has a son who is a dentist. She always has many interesting and amusing little stories to tell. This one is a favourite of mine.

An elderly lady had her regular check-up with her dentist. As he finished his exam the dentist pronounced, "Mrs. Smith, your teeth are good for the next fifty years."

With a smile and a sigh, Mrs. Smith replied, "I wonder what they'll do without me!"

February

White Fields

IN the winter time we go
Walking in the fields of snow;

Where there is no grass at all;
Where the top of every wall,

Every fence and every tree,
Is as white as white can be.

Pointing out the way we came,
— Every one of them the same —

All across the fields there be
Prints in silver filigree;

And our mothers always know,
By the footprints in the snow,
Where it is the children go.

— James Stephens

THE HERITAGE BOOK

TODAY is always a welcome chance for we "serious" Canadians to poke a little fun at ourselves and at our long winters.

"Groundhog Day" is celebrated in Canada each February second. On this day, weathermen on both radio and television report to us, very seriously, as to whether or not "Wiarton Willie" (an ordinary Canadian groundhog) has seen his shadow. If such be the case, the groundhog will return to his burrow to wait out six more weeks of winter.

This "vital" news is eagerly awaited by tens of thousands of interested Canadians.

LIVING God, in Christ you make all things new, transform the poverty of our nature by the riches of your grace, and in the renewal of our lives make known your glory, through Jesus Christ our Lord, who is alive and reigns with you and the Holy Spirit, one God, now and forever.

Amen.
Fourth Sunday of the Epiphany
— Book of Alternative Services

THE HERITAGE BOOK

ALTHOUGH skiing is a very popular sport, there are people who have other ideas on this winter activity. One of these is Erma Bombeck, a popular writer of our times. When asked to participate in a pro-am charity ski race, she responded, "I do not participate in any sport with ambulances at the bottom of the hill."

UNLESS they share our opinions, we seldom find people sensible.
— *Duc de la Rochefoucauld*

ONE of life's greatest pleasures is doing what someone has said could never be done.

THE HERITAGE BOOK

As my former readers are aware, I have been taking piano lessons for the past few years.

Many of my friends were both amused and perplexed at my decision to begin lessons at such an advanced age. "What a silly notion!" was the common response. How happy I am that I accepted the support of my family and overcame my own misgivings to embark on this most enjoyable and satisfying of pursuits.

My teacher, a wonderfully gifted instructor, has been able to impart enough knowledge that I may now sit down at the keyboard and play, if not perfectly, well enough that the music is enjoyable to listen to.

This evening was a real highlight in my "musical career." Marg and Bruce had entertained several old friends for dinner, and as we enjoyed our coffee, Marg asked me to show off my skills.

At first I was nervous and reluctant, but with a little coaxing I relented. As I started to play, everything and everyone around me seemed to disappear and I was caught up in the sound of my music. I was brought back by the applause and warm congratulations of our friends.

It was indeed a proud moment.

FRIDAY — FEBRUARY 8

To be content, look backward on those who possess less than yourself, not forward to those who possess more. If this does not make you content, you don't deserve to be happy.

— *Benjamin Franklin*

SATURDAY — FEBRUARY 9

No man can hold another in the gutter without remaining there himself.

— *Booker T. Washington*

SUNDAY — FEBRUARY 10

That evening, at sundown, they brought to Jesus all who were sick and possessed with demons — and he healed many. And in the morning, a great while before day, he rose and went out to a lonely place, and there he prayed.

— *Mark 1:32-35*

THE HERITAGE BOOK

Marg and Bruce suffered the loss of a very close friend this weekend. Jim had waged a valiant battle against cancer and although his death came as a blessed relief from his suffering, it was, nonetheless, a tragic loss to his family and his many friends.

I hope this prayer will be of some small comfort to them this evening.

Grant, O Lord, to all who are bereaved, the spirit of faith and courage, that they may have the strength to meet the days to come with steadfastness and patience; not sorrowing as those without hope, but in thankful remembrance of thy great goodness in past years, and in the sure expectation of a joyful reunion in the heavenly places; and this we ask in the name of Jesus Christ our Lord.

— *Irish Prayer Book*

TUESDAY — FEBRUARY 12

WE love old cathedrals, old furniture, old silver, old dictionaries and old prints, but we have entirely forgotten about the beauty of old men. I think an appreciation of that kind of beauty is essential to our life; for beauty, it seems to me, is what is old and mellow and well smoked.

— *Lin Yutang*

WEDNESDAY — FEBRUARY 13
Ash Wednesday

THIS is the day for self-examination in the presence of God the Spirit — and a day for beginning afresh some resolve to grow in faith, to renew our hope and discover new ways of expressing the love we experience through our community of believers.

Many of the older customs associated with Lent have changed. From an "oldster's" point of view they have become more open and challenging. The new ideas provide fresh thought about an ancient faith.

May we use these forty days wisely in faith and friendship.

THE HERITAGE BOOK

THIS is a happy day for all those who are in love. St. Valentine's Day is a wonderful time to show those we love how special we think they are.

A card, flowers, or a special dinner are just a few of the ways to show this caring.

Time is . . .
Too slow for those who wait,
Too swift for those who fear,
Too long for those who grieve,
Too short for those who rejoice;
But for those who love, time is eternity.
— *Henry Van Dyke*

I LIKE the man who, whenever he encountered the question "RACE" in a visa application, answered with the word "HUMAN."

SATURDAY — FEBRUARY 16

CONSISTENCY is the last refuge of the unimaginative.

— *Oscar Wilde*

SUNDAY — FEBRUARY 17
First Sunday in Lent

O GOD, you are my God. I seek Thee early with a heart that thirsts for Thee, and a body wasted with longing for Thee like a dry and thirsty land that has no water. So, longing, I come before Thee in the Sanctuary to look upon Thy power and glory. Thy true love is better than life, therefore I will sing thy promises.

— *Psalms 63:1-3*

MONDAY — FEBRUARY 18

AN old Spanish proverb says "Self-knowledge is the beginning of self-improvement."

MY dear friend Emily wrote from the sunny south this week. In her letter she describes the beautiful weather and the great pleasures of walking the beach each day.

"I enjoy my daily walks so much, Edna. On the hot and sunny days I wear my bathing suit, my sun hat and lots of sunscreen. Usually there are many people sunning, swimming, or shell hunting. On these days I enjoy watching the children as they scamper into the shallow water to pick out the shells washing up on the shore. Their excitement is contagious and soon the adults become caught up in finding the 'savers' as well.

But it's the cool days that I enjoy most. Often I am the only person in sight for miles; the pelicans, the sandpipers and the breakers are my only companions. The enormity of the ocean gives one such a feeling of awe. My thoughts become clearer and all my worries seem to disappear.

The peace gained is a great joy."

THE HERITAGE BOOK

M Y friend Jake Frampton, an avid reader, found this interesting bit of information in an old newspaper.

The police force in Sri Lanka found an interesting method of increasing the income of policemen's families while reducing the cost of uniforms. The Police Families' Welfare Association hired the wives and children of policemen to sew the men's uniforms. Paid on a daily basis, the wives and children produced 40,000 uniforms a year. The program was so successful that the army was considering a similar set-up.

W E should so live and labour in our time that what came to us as seed may go to the next generation as blossom, and that which came to us as blossom may go to them as fruit.
— *Henry Ward Beecher*

T HE man who makes no mistakes does not usually make anything.
— *Edward John Phelps*

THE HERITAGE BOOK

THIS afternoon I enjoyed watching figure skating on the afternoon T.V. sport program. Of the many winter sports telecasts, I believe that figure skating is my very favourite.

Figure skating has advanced dramatically over the past years. I can remember watching Sonja Henie, Dick Button, and Canada's own Barbara Ann Scott and Donald Jackson as they performed at various world championships. At the time I recall thinking, "It can never get better than this."

Now, of course, skaters are able to perform difficult triple jumps and even "quadruples," and their programs have been choreographed to perfection. The skaters today are such finely-tuned athletes that their feats appear to be almost commonplace.

Of all of the competitions, I prefer the "ice dance." Perhaps it is because it is one area that I find easy to identify with. George and I often spent a Saturday afternoon in the old arena skating to music played by the arena organist. In my mind's eye I can visualize George and I performing as these young dancers do. Imagination is a wonderful thing.

THE HERITAGE BOOK

A BRIEF meditation based on Psalm 63 for the second Sunday in Lent.

Eternal God, our hearts are restless until they rest in you. Let your glory shine on us, that our lives may proclaim your goodness, our work give you honour, and our voices praise you forever, for the sake of Jesus Christ our Lord.

Amen.

—*Book of Alternative Service*

O LDER people on a fixed income often find that the old barter system is an excellent way to make ends meet.

My friend John, a wonderful gardener, often has his minor car repairs done in exchange for a few hours of work in the mechanic's garden. The mechanic, who lacks a green thumb, was delighted with the exchange.

One day in early summer, John walked into the service station and said, "Mike, my car has a problem. I think it's probably worth a dozen prize rose bushes and a large vegetable garden!"

A UTHORITY without wisdom is like a heavy axe without an edge, fitter to bruise than polish.

— *Anne Bradstreet*

WEDNESDAY — FEBRUARY 27

In February

N ow in the dark of February rains,
Poor lovers of the sunshine, spring is born,
The earthy fields are full of hidden corn,
And March's violets bud along the lanes.
Therefore with joy believe in what remains.
And thou who dost not feel them, do not scorn
Our early songs for winter overworn,
And faith in God's handwriting on the plains.

'Hope,' writes he, 'Love' in the first violet,
'Joy,' even from Heaven, in songs and winds and trees;
And having caught the happy words in these
While Nature labours with the letters yet,
Spring cannot cheat us, though her hopes be broken,
Nor leave us, for we know what God hath spoken.

— *George MacDonald*

THE HERITAGE BOOK

I MUST confess that I am happy to see the end of February. Although it is a short month, the cold weather and long hours of darkness make February feel like a much longer month than it really is.

I look forward to the month of March, when Spring may be welcomed back once more.

Let us hope to say, "farewell snow and freezing weather; farewell grey days and long nights; farewell February."

March

IF you sit down at set of sun
And count the acts that you have done,
And, counting, find
One self-denying deed, one word
That eased the heart of him who heard —
One glance most kind,
That fell like sunshine where it went —
Then you may count that day well spent.
— *George Eliot*

THE best educated human being is the one
who understands most about the life in
which he is placed.
— *Helen Keller*

SUNDAY — MARCH 3
Third Sunday in Lent

THE heavens declare the glory of God
And the firmament show his handiworks,
One day tells its tale to another, and one night
imparts knowledge to another.

Although they have no words or language
and their voices are not heard, the sound has
gone out into all lands and their message to the
end of the world.

— *Psalm 19:1-4*

MONDAY — MARCH 4

MY daughter Julia spent the past weekend
visiting with us.

As an executive with an international company, she is required to travel extensively.
Most recently her work took her to Australia
and New Zealand.

Marg, Bruce, and I were treated to many
wonderful slides of some of the more beautiful
areas of Australia, and of the many unusual
animals that inhabit those areas. Kangaroos,
kiwis, and koalas were featured in many of her
photos. I was amazed by the size of the koalas
and their baby-like faces as they seemed to
smile at the camera. I felt as if I had been to
Australia — and I hope to go again.

THE HERITAGE BOOK

TUESDAY — MARCH 5

FAITH is not belief without proof; it is trust without reservation.

— *Martin Hulsemann*

WEDNESDAY — MARCH 6

THERE are nine requisites for contented living: health enough to make work a pleasure; wealth enough to support your needs; strength to battle with difficulties and overcome them; grace enough to confess your sins and forsake them; patience enough to toil until some good is accomplished; charity enough to see some good in your neighbour; love enough to move you to be useful and helpful to others; faith enough to make real the things of God; hope enough to remove all anxious fears concerning the future.

— *Goethe*

THURSDAY — MARCH 7

WE are never so generous as when giving advice.

— *Duc de la Rochefoucauld*

THE HERITAGE BOOK

TODAY is the birthday of my son-in-law Bruce. Marg had decided several weeks ago to have a small get-together with some close friends to celebrate the occasion. The invitations were sent with the added note "Please — no gifts."

It was with surprise, then, that Marg and Bruce opened the door to the first guest who arrived carrying a large and heavy gift-wrapped box. Their surprise was greater as every couple appeared with beautifully wrapped boxes, seemingly ignoring Marg's "no gifts" request.

When all of the invited guests had arrived, all bearing gifts, John Mason, a close friend of Bruce's, explained the mystery.

"We knew that you really meant what you said when you asked that we not give you gifts. However, we wanted to do something special so we bought gifts that we thought would be appropriate for nursing home residents. We are going to deliver these gifts in your name to 'The Manor,' and maybe some others can enjoy your birthday as well."

THE HERITAGE BOOK

OUR good friend and neighbour Lila McGuiness has come down with a terrible cold. Marg and I decided to make chicken soup, our favourite cold "antidote." I thought that some of you might enjoy our recipe. (Makes about 2 quarts.)

1	4-lb. chicken
3 quarts	cold water
2	carrots, peeled and chopped
2	celery stalks, chopped
1	large onion, chopped
1 clove	garlic
3 tbsp	chopped parsley
1 tsp	salt
	pepper to taste

Wash the chicken thoroughly, then cut into parts. Place the chicken in a large pot and cover with the water. Bring to a boil; cook approximately 30 minutes, then skim the fat off the top. Add the remaining ingredients, cover, and simmer slowly for about 2 1/2 hours, or until the chicken is tender.

Remove chicken and bones; chop chicken in small pieces. If you prefer, the vegetables may be strained out (I like to leave the vegetables in). Put chicken pieces in the pot again. Serve.

SUNDAY — MARCH 10
Fourth Sunday in Lent

CREATOR and ruler of all, open our hearts that the King of Glory may enter, and bring us rejoicing to your holy mountain, where you live and reign now and forever.
> — *Meditation based on Psalm 24*
> *Book of Alternative Services*

MONDAY — MARCH 11

COMMON sense is the most widely distributed commodity in the world, for everyone thinks himself so well endowed with it that those who are hardest to please in any other respect generally have no desire to possess more of it than they have.
> — *René Descartes*

TUESDAY — MARCH 12

THERE is no use worrying about things over which you have no control, and if you have control, you can do something about them instead of worrying!

THE HERITAGE BOOK

THE primary school in our area has several French immersion classes, and the Grade 1 teacher passed on this amusing story to me.

Each morning the national anthem is played over the P.A. system into every classroom. It is an instrumental version and each class group sings along with the music.

In the immersion classes, the children sing along in French. In the Grade 1 class this is the first version of the anthem that they have been taught, so many of the children assume that all people sing the anthem this way.

This was brought to light one morning when one of the young students happened to be standing out in the hall near the English Grade 1 class. As the anthem played, Jed dutifully sang, but as the music went on and he listened to the class singing the English version of the anthem, he faltered, and finally stopped. As it finished, he rushed into his own room and announced, "Madame, you'd better go and help the class down the hall. Those poor kids don't even know the words to the anthem — I don't know *what* they were singing!"

To My Sister

IT is the first mild day of March;
Each minute sweeter than before,
The redbreast sings from the tall larch
That stands beside our door.

There is a blessing in the air,
Which seems a sense of joy to yield
To the bare trees, and mountains bare,
And grass in the green field.
— *William Wordsworth*

BERNARD Baruch made an interesting obser-
vation: "I will never be an old man. To me
old age is always fifteen years older than I
am."

THE HERITAGE BOOK

LITTLE drops of water,
Little grains of sand,
Make the mighty ocean
And the pleasant land.

So the little minutes,
Humble though they be,
Make the mighty ages
Of eternity.

This poem from Julia Fletcher Carney is a reminder to all of us that time is precious. As I advance in years, this fact becomes more and more apparent to me.

As children we often wished time away. "When I'm six I can have a real bicycle." "I wish I were in high school now." "I wish I were finished school." And so on. Do you remember?

As children we feel immortal. As seniors we feel our mortality all too well as time flies by.

Constructive use of the time allotted to us may be our only way of slowing time's fleet passing.

It is said that the average person fritters away enough minutes in ten years to earn a college degree. Let's earn that degree.

SUNDAY — MARCH 17

Passion Sunday

I WILL lift up my eyes to the hills
Whence shall I find help
Help comes only from the Lord
Maker of heaven and earth.

— *Psalm 121*

MONDAY — MARCH 18

YESTERDAY was St. Patrick's Day, celebrated by all Irishmen (as well as by those who would like to claim an Irish heritage).

My father was of Irish descent and was very proud of it. This very old rune, said to have been spoken by St. Patrick on his way to Tara, was a favourite of my father's:

I arise today . . .
Through the strength of heaven:
Light of sun,
Radiance of moon,
Splendour of fire,
Speed of lightning,
Swiftness of wind,
Depth of sea,
Stability of earth,
Firmness of rock.

THE HERITAGE BOOK

SEVERAL years ago, I read an article by Robert Fulghum in the *Kansas City Times*. In it, Mr. Fulghum said that most of what he really needed to know about how to live and how to be he learned in Kindergarten.

These are the things he learned: Share. Play fair. Don't hit people. Put things back where you found them. Clean up your own mess. Don't take things that aren't yours. Say you're sorry when you hurt somebody. Wash your hands before you eat. Warm cookies and cold milk are good for you. Live a balanced life. Learn some and think some, and draw and paint and sing and dance and play and work some every day.

Take a nap in the afternoon. When you go out into the world, watch for traffic, hold hands, and stick together. Be aware of wonder. Remember the little seed in the plastic cup. The roots go down and the plant goes up and nobody really knows why, but we are all like that.

Goldfish, hamsters, white mice, even the little seed in the cup — they all die. So do we.

WEDNESDAY — MARCH 20

LIVE so you wouldn't be ashamed to sell the family parrot to the town gossip.

— *Will Rogers*

THURSDAY — MARCH 21

THE best way to appreciate your job is to imagine yourself without it.

FRIDAY — MARCH 22

WHAT lovelier way to begin spring than with the words from The Song of Solomon II : 11-12:

"For lo, the winter is past, the rain is over and gone, the flowers appear on the earth; the time of the singing of birds is come, and the voice of the turtle is heard in our land."

SATURDAY — MARCH 23

M<small>Y</small> dear friends Will and Muriel stopped in for a visit today, bringing with them a lovely touch of spring. Gracing my coffee table is a magnificent basket of blooming daffodils.

Back in the early winter, Will stored many dozens of daffodil and tulip bulbs in pots in the cold room of his basement. Some weeks before he wanted the dormant bulbs to sprout, he removed them from their cold storage and placed them in his greenhouse room under warm lamps.

The result is my beautiful "welcome" to spring.

SUNDAY — MARCH 24
Palm Sunday

T<small>HE</small> Lord is my shepherd; I shall not want. He maketh me to lie down in green pastures; he leadeth me beside the still waters. He restoreth my soul: he leadeth me in the paths of righteousness for his name's sake. Yea though I walk through the valley of the shadow of death I will fear no evil; for thou art with me; thy rod and thy staff they comfort me.

— Psalm 23:1-4

THE HERITAGE BOOK

MONDAY — MARCH 25

THE happiest moments my heart knows are those in which it is pouring forth its affections to a few esteemed characters.

— *Thomas Jefferson*

TUESDAY — MARCH 26

THE heart that is truly happy never grows old. We don't cease playing because we have grown old; we grow old because we have ceased playing.

WEDNESDAY — MARCH 27

IF you have accomplished all that you have planned for yourself, you have not planned enough.

THURSDAY — MARCH 28

Don't flatter yourself that friendship authorizes you to say disagreeable things to your intimates. On the contrary, the nearer you come into relationship with a person the more necessary do tact and courtesy become. Except in cases of necessity, which are rare, let your friend learn unpleasant truths from his enemies — they are usually ready to tell him.

— Oliver Wendell Holmes

FRIDAY — MARCH 29
Good Friday

Almighty God, the Father of all mankind, we pray to thee to turn to thyself the hearts of all peoples and their rulers, that by the power of the Holy Spirit, peace may be established on the foundation of justice, righteousness and truth through Him who was lifted up on the Cross to draw all men unto Himself, even thy son, Jesus Christ our Lord.

Amen.

— William Temple

THE HERITAGE BOOK

ISN'T it interesting how times change? Many years ago on this day before Easter, our family would be scurrying about gathering together all of our fine clothing to wear to church on Easter Sunday. This always included a hat, usually new, and white gloves. New hats for Easter were a tradition in our community and most likely in every community across Canada and North America.

In recent times hats fell from favour and it became quite rare to see a hat on anyone but those more elderly ladies of the congregation.

Then came Princess Diana with her fantastic collection of "chapeaux," and suddenly hats, and gloves, are back in style.

My granddaughter Phyllis spent today at a nearby mall with Jenny, and the two of them stopped by to model their new ensembles for tomorrow.

You guessed it. Both Jenny and her mother have new white gloves and fashionable straw hats with flowers.

"The more things change the more they stay the same."

THE HERITAGE BOOK

Easter Sunday

A DAY of Triumph — Blessed are you, strong shepherd of your people. You hear us when we lift our hands and our hearts in prayer. And through your son, Jesus Christ our Lord, you give us the promise of eternal inheritance. Blessed are you forever.

Amen.

— Book of Alternative Services

April

THIS is the special day for the practical jokers in our society, during which they can let their imaginations run to outrageous pranks to play on unsuspecting friends.

I don't usually enjoy practical jokes, but I did get a good laugh from Jake Frampton's "April Fool" story.

Jake and his friend John often tried to "get" one another with all manner of elaborate tricks.

Several years ago the two men were in the woods of northern Ontario on a photography expedition.

"Oh Lord, don't move!" Jake cried. "There's a bear right behind you."

John, remembering that it was April Fool's Day, laughed and replied, "Come on, Jake, you can do better than that." As he spoke he turned his head slightly, and to his immense surprise he was almost face to face with a brown bear.

The two men fled and the bear, slow after a winter of hibernation, made no move to follow.

THE HERITAGE BOOK

I AM fortunate to have many people whom I consider to be good friends.

Today I offer to you others' ideas on friends and friendship.

A friend may well be reckoned the masterpiece of nature.

— *Ralph Waldo Emerson*

A constant friend is a thing rare and hard to find.

— *Plutarch*

Friendship is a sheltering tree.

— *Samuel Taylor Coleridge*

Friendship improves happiness, and abates misery, by doubling our joy, and dividing our grief.

— *Joseph Addison*

Hold a true friend with both your hands.

— *Nigerian Proverb*

THE HERITAGE BOOK

Back in 1936, Wendell Wilkie, then president of Commonwealth and Southern Corporation, was at a convention in Atlanta, Georgia. One of the delegates told him, "The last time you were here I introduced you to my wife. Do you remember her? Well, she's written a book that has been accepted by a publisher. If it sells enough copies to earn her five thousand dollars, we are going to buy a new house."

"Good for her!" Mr. Wilkie was most enthusiastic as he went on. "I have never done anything like this before, but I'm going to write a letter to every stockholder, signed by me, urging him to buy a copy of your wife's book."

He did exactly that and for many years he would laughingly declare that he deserved some of the credit for getting the book off to a rousing start.

The book's name? *Gone With the Wind.*

When someone says, "I'm telling you this for your own good," you probably aren't going to enjoy hearing it.

It's easy to find reasons why other folks should be patient.

— *George Eliot*

A. A. MILNE once wrote, "The average man finds life very uninteresting as it is. And I think that the reason why is that he is always waiting for something to happen to him instead of setting to work to make things happen. For one person who dreams of making fifty thousand pounds, a hundred people dream of being left fifty thousand pounds."

Jesus said "Set your troubled hearts at rest. Trust in God always, trust also in me. There are many dwelling places in my Father's house. If it were not so I would have told you, for I am going there on purpose to prepare a place for you."

— *John 14:1-2*

THE HERITAGE BOOK

IT'S the little things in life that count,
The things of every day;
Just the simple things that we can do,
The kind words we can say.
The little things like a friendly smile
For those who may be sad,
The clasp of a hand or kindly deed
To help make someone glad.
A knock on the door of lonely homes,
Or flowers bright and gay,
For someone to whom you might bring cheer
With just a small bouquet.
Just the little greetings here and there
On which so much depends,
The little pleasures that all can share,
The joy of making friends.

—Virginia Katherine Oliver

LET me be a little kinder,
Let me be a little blinder,
To the faults of those around me,
Let me praise a little more.

— Edgar A. Guest

WEDNESDAY — APRIL 10

THE deeper man goes into life, the deeper is his conviction that this life is not all; it is an "unfinished symphony." A day may round out an insect's life, and a bird or a beast needs no tomorrow. Not so with him who knows that he is related to God and has felt the power of an endless life.

— Henry Ward Beecher

THURSDAY — APRIL 11

THE older I get the more I realize there is but one wealth, one security on this earth and that is found in the ability of a person to perform a task well. And first and foremost, this ability must start with knowledge.

— Abraham Lincoln

FRIDAY — APRIL 12

ONE thing that we learn the hard way is that there is no easy way.

WITH the baseball season just under way, I thought you might enjoy this story about two of the game's legends.

Back in 1931 in Chattanooga, Tennessee, the fantastic New York Yankees played the Chattanooga Lookouts in an exhibition game. The Chattanooga team included a 17-year-old pitcher — Virnie Beatrice "Jackie" Mitchell, a left-handed fast-ball pitcher from Fall River, Massachusetts.

Promoter Joe Engel, quick to see the potential in a "girl vs. the Yankees" confrontation, signed her to his team in an effort to fill his stadium for the game.

A packed house was there to see Jackie face Babe Ruth at bat in the first inning.

The first pitch blazed in. Ruth took a mighty swing — and missed. The next two pitches were wide. Jackie wound up, threw a fastball; Ruth swung and missed. The count was now 2 balls, 2 strikes. On her final throw, Ruth didn't move the bat as the umpire yelled "Strike three — you're out!" The Babe walked away shaking his head. Next up was Lou Gehrig. He wasted no time. He swung at Jackie's first three balls — and missed them all.

Jackie was "The girl who struck out Babe Ruth."

THE HERITAGE BOOK

A s Jesus was stepping into the boat, the man who had been possessed begged to go with him. "Go home to your own folk and tell them what the Lord, in his mercy, has done for you."

— Mark 5:18-19

F OR many years I have enjoyed doing crossword puzzles. Each night as I prepared dinner, my husband George would sit at the kitchen table and work on the crossword in the evening paper. Every so often he would say "Edna, do you know a four-letter word for an African fox?" or "Who composed *Pomp and Circumstance*?"

More often than not I had absolutely no idea of the answers, but as George did more and more puzzles, I began to remember some of the more bizarre questions and answers. After dinner, when George would retire to his desk to work, I would try to finish the puzzles.

Now my day doesn't seem complete until I have done the evening crossword. Say, do you know a six-letter word . . .

A FTER you have exhausted what there is in business, politics, conviviality and so on — have found that none of these finally satisfy, or permanently wear — what remains? Nature remains.

— *Walt Whitman*

T HIS morning I saw two robins on my lawn and Emily Dickinson's poem "Robin" came immediately to mind.

The robin is the one
That interrupts the morn
With hurried, few, express reports
When March is scarcely on.

The robin is the one
That overflows the noon
With her cherubic quantity,
An April but begun.

The robin is the one
That speechless from her nest
Submits that home and certainty
And sanctity are best.

THE HERITAGE BOOK

"LISTEN my children, and you shall hear
Of the midnight ride of Paul Revere."

How many of you history buffs, reading these lines from Henry Wadsworth Longfellow's famous poem, remember that today is the anniversary of Paul Revere's famous ride?

Paul Revere was an American patriot and craftsman. Born in Boston of French Huguenot ancestry on January 1, 1735, he learned the silversmith's trade. He also drew political cartoons that were used as effective propoganda by the rebellious colonials.

Revere participated in the Boston Tea Party of 1773 and rode horseback to New York to inform the Sons of Liberty of this event. Subsequent missions earned him the title of "Official Courier to the Continental Congress."

Several days before his most famous ride, he made an equally important ride to warn the patriots to move their military stores from Concord. At this time he arranged his famous "one if by land, two if by sea" signal in reference to the lights to be placed in North Church steeple to warn of the British approach. The ride to Lexington on this date in 1775 changed the course of history.

THE HERITAGE BOOK

I AM always content with that which happens, for I think that which God chooses is better than what I choose.

— *Epictetus*

IT is a fine thing to have ability, but the ability to discover ability in others is the true test.

—*Elbert Hubbard*

FOR the beauty of the earth
For the glory of the skies
For the love which from our birth
Over and around us lies
Lord of all to thee we raise
This our sacrifice of praise.

— *Folliott Sandford Pierpoint*

THE HERITAGE BOOK

MONDAY — APRIL 22

FOURTH graders in a class for gifted children were asked by their teacher to complete a sentence beginning "Let's be as quiet as . . ."

Here are some of their answers: ". . . a soft breeze . . . time passing . . . a gentle rainfall . . . when you pray . . . a leaf turning colours . . . a feather falling from a bird . . . the first star coming out . . . a butterfly flying."

TUESDAY — APRIL 23

A WISE person once said "There are only two lasting bequests we can hope to give our children. One of these is roots; the other, wings."

WEDNESDAY — APRIL 24

APOLOGIZING for a nasty remark is like trying to unscramble an egg.

THURSDAY — APRIL 25

ALTHOUGH Canada is officially a bilingual country, many of our politicians mangle the French language. They would do well to use Clare Boothe Luce's favourite line when she began to practise speaking Italian to Italians: "I am now going to try to talk in a language that's not mine. And when I do, you'll probably think it's not yours either!"

FRIDAY — APRIL 26

WHAT a delight to spend time in the out of doors! The fine weather of the past few days has lured me to walk much farther and longer than I have been able to since last fall.

How pleasant to see crocus blooming and shoots of daffodils and tulips springing up in gardens.

How nice, too, to hear the birds twittering as they flit about searching for twigs and bits of string for their nests.

This truly is a time of renewal. At the end of the long winter the promise of new life is once more fulfilled, and I, for one, am grateful.

THE HERITAGE BOOK

IF we learn how to give of ourselves, to forgive others, and to live with thanksgiving, we need not seek happiness — it will seek us.

ALMIGHTY God, your son Jesus Christ is the way, the truth and the life; give us grace to love one another and walk in the way of his commandments who lives and reigns with you and the Holy Spirit. One God, now and forever.

Amen.
— *Book of Alternative Services*

IT is those who have a deep and real inner life who are best able to deal with the irritating details of outer life.
— *Evelyn Underhill*

M Y grandson Marshall and I had a good laugh today. He brought a list of auto insurance claims that his agent had sent for his enjoyment.

"I pulled away from the side of the road, glanced at my mother-in-law, and headed over the embankment."

"In my attempt to kill a fly I drove into a telephone pole."

"I had been driving my car for forty years when I fell asleep at the wheel and had an accident."

"I told police that I was not injured, but on removing my hat I found that I had a skull fracture."

May

Now the bright morning Star, Dayes harbinger
Comes dancing from the East, and leads with her
The Flowery May, who from her green lap throws
The Yellow Cowslip and the pale Primrose.
Hail bounteous May! thou dost inspire Mirth, and youth and warm desire;
Woods and Groves are of the dressing;
Hill and Dale doth boast thy blessing.
Thus we salute thee with our early Song,
And welcome thee, and wish thee long.
— *John Milton*

THE HERITAGE BOOK

MORE and more Canadians are discovering the joys of tape-recorded books that let you "read" with your ears.

The original intent of audio books was to allow people with deteriorating eyesight (or no vision at all) to enjoy great literary works.

People of all ages have discovered that it is now possible to "read" while their eyes are otherwise occupied. It can be a joy to be stuck in traffic as you listen to Lee Iacocca's autobiography. Gardening, sewing, cooking, may all be done as master storytellers enthrall us with imaginative narrations.

The selection now available is remarkable — there are at least 15,000 titles of short works, and 5000 word-for-word recordings of full-length books, ranging from the classics to modern "best-sellers."

Because of costs, most publishers produce works that will fit on two cassettes (for about three hours of listening).

Many of the narrators are well known: Katherine Hepburn, Dick Cavett, Richard Crenna, and James Herriot, to name but a few.

For anyone who has ever said "I wish I had more time to read," it is a wish come true.

THE HERITAGE BOOK

Now is the high-tide of the year,
    And whatever of life hath ebbed away
Comes flooding back with a ripply cheer,
Into every bare inlet and creek and bay;
Now the heart is so full that a drop overfills it,
We are happy now because God wills it,
No matter how barren the past may have been
'Tis enough for us now that the leaves are
    green . . .

— *James Russell Lowell*

THE difference between a prejudice and a conviction is that you can explain a conviction without getting mad.

GOD has told you what is good — and what is it that the Lord asks of you? Only to act justly, to love loyalty, to walk wisely before your God.

— *Micah 6:8*

MONDAY — MAY 6

THIS is a wonderful time of year to visit the orchards of the Niagara region.

Yesterday, Marg, Bruce and I made just such a visit on a beautiful Sunday drive following our morning church service.

Instead of taking the highway, Bruce chose to drive on the back roads, many of which are of the dirt and gravel variety. As we passed the fruit trees on the farm properties of the area, my breath was taken away by the beauty of the blossoms.

The pink and white blossom-covered branches, as well as those of mauve or red, foretell of an abundant harvest to come.

"While the earth remaineth seed time and harvest shall not fail" is God's promise to us.

TUESDAY — MAY 7

IF I can put one touch of a rosy sunset into the life of any man or woman, I shall feel that I have worked with God.

— *Henry David Thoreau*

WEDNESDAY — MAY 8

WHEN parents do too much for their children, the children will not do much for themselves.

— *Elbert Hubbard*

THURSDAY — MAY 9

OUR memory is like a sieve, the holes of which, in time, get larger and larger; the older we get, the quicker anything entrusted to it slips from the memory, whereas what was fixed fast to it in early days is still there. The memory of an old man gets clearer and clearer the further it goes back, and less clear the nearer it approaches the present time so that his memory, like his eyes, becomes far-sighted.

— *Schopenhauer*

FRIDAY — MAY 10

CHARM is that quality in others of making us more satisfied with ourselves.

— *Frederic Amiel*

THE HERITAGE BOOK

COMING together is a beginning; keeping together is progress; working together is success.

— *Henry Ford*

I HOPE you have the opportunity on Mother's Day, as we do in our parish church, to renew your sense of belonging to a larger family. Our pastor feels strongly that the important note for today is Christian Family Life.

As a part of the celebration there is usually a service of Baptism. This morning six infants, with parents and god-parents, came with their families to be received into the church of Christ and to receive the gift of the Holy Spirit for their Christian growth.

Like many others I use this service as a time of renewal of my vows of baptism. It is a time to remember that I am not travelling the journey of faith alone but with a community of believers. It is good to be a part of the larger "Family of Faith."

THE HERITAGE BOOK

LIFE has loveliness to sell,
All beautiful and splendid things,
Blue waves whitened on a cliff,
Soaring fire that sways and sings,
And children's faces looking up
Holding wonder like a cup.

Life has loveliness to sell,
Music like a curve of gold,
Scent of pine trees in the rain,
Eyes that love you, arms that hold,
And for your spirits still delight,
Holy thoughts that star the night.

Spend all you have for loveliness,
Buy it and never count the cost;
For one white singing hour of peace
Count many a year of strife well lost,
And for a breath of ecstasy
Give all you have been, or could be.
— *Sara Teasdale*

THE worst sin towards our fellow creatures
is not to hate them, but to be indifferent to
them: that's the essence of inhumanity.
— *Bernard Shaw*

THE HERITAGE BOOK

A GROUP of us "oldies" got together for a social evening recently. As often happens, our conversation turned to the subject of grandchildren and great-grandchildren.

In our discussion we offered our views on what makes a *great* grandparent. Not surprisingly, many of us had similar viewpoints. I offer to you today our thoughts on "grand grandparents."

Invite the family over very regularly for dinners. Three generations getting together has a positive effect on all.

Holidays are an excellent time for family get-togethers. These times provide wonderful memories that the grandchildren will keep with them all their lives.

Don't be a parent to your grandchildren. It is their parents' job to discipline. The grandparents' job is to indulge and even to spoil them a little.

Make it a ritual to tell them about your youth and their parent's youth. This gives them a good sense of family history.

When possible, baby-sit regularly. This gives children an excellent sense of security.

Most of all love them. Children need this more than anything else — and so do we.

IF one advances confidently in the direction of his dreams, and endeavours to live the life which he has imagined, he will meet with a success unexpected in common hours.

— *Henry David Thoreau*

EXPERIENCE is the name everyone gives to his mistakes.

— *Oscar Wilde*

MANY china shops have posted the following verse: "Lovely to look at, delightful to hold, but if you should break it, consider it sold." My friend Jake Frampton told me of a slightly different verse in the giftware store next to his book shop.

"Nice to look at, nicer to hold, but if you break it you will receive five free kittens!"

SUNDAY — MAY 19
Pentecost Sunday

WHILE the Day of Pentecost was running its course they were all together in one place, when suddenly there came from the sky a noise like that of a strong driving wind which filled the whole house where they were sitting. And there appeared to them tongues as of fire, which dispersed among them and rested on each one. And they were all filled with the Holy Spirit.

— Acts 2:1-4

MONDAY — MAY 20

TODAY Marg, Bruce and I are in Muskoka. It is our annual weekend outing in this lovely area where we help my dear friend Eleanor to open her cottage for the season.

In spite of the cool weather there were many boats out on the water taking advantage of the sun on the waves. After our chores were done we sat around the fire with a hot cup of tea and remembered when cottage opening was a long and odious task. I think that now is the "good old days."

PETER Sellers, that zany actor of "Pink Panther" film fame, had a favourite pastime — making odd remarks to be overheard in hotel elevators.

He and a good friend had one conversation that would begin this way: "Outrageous to see a corpse wheeled out of a room in a first-class hotel like this one."

Another favourite was "Did you feed the gorilla? Are you sure he'll be alright in the room alone?"

Or, "You can't drink. Why don't you get help? Don't tell me you are going to operate like this! You can hardly stand up!"

PEOPLE who are always trying to get even can hardly expect to get ahead.

A CONSCIENCE, like a buzzing bee, can make a fellow uneasy without ever stinging him.

THE HERITAGE BOOK

PRINCESS Alexandrina Victoria was born on this day in 1819. In 1837, one month after her 18th birthday, she became Queen of England. She was to be the longest-reigning British monarch, ruling until her death on January 22, 1901.

Her good common sense and directness of character made her a beloved monarch, truly worthy of the title of Her Majesty, Queen Victoria.

So live — decently, fearlessly, joyously — and don't forget that it is not the years in your life but the life in your years that counts.

HOLY, Holy, Holy! Lord God Almighty!
Early in the morning our song shall rise to Thee
Holy, Holy, Holy! Merciful and mighty,
God in Three Persons, Blessed Trinity.
— *Bishop R. Heber*

THE HERITAGE BOOK

Any of you who have suffered "strep throat" — a streptococcus infection causing a severe sore throat — and who have been given the antibiotic tetracycline may find this story of interest.

Dr. Ben Duggar, a botany professor, was 70 years old in 1943 when the University of Wisconsin told him he was through. Though Dr. Duggar protested that he was "a young 70," the university had a rule that retirement was mandatory at 70. Duggar had to step down. The decision of the faculty caused him great pain.

A few of Duggar's graduates were working at Lederle Laboratories. They spoke to the top boss at Lederle and Ben Duggar was hired as a consultant and independent researcher.

In the Lederle labs were thousands of small drawers with samples of earth from all over the world. They needed to be cross-matched and nurtured into growing molds. This meant nearly 36 million cross-matchings. After an uneventful first year, he isolated the antibiotic aureomycin. From this he got tetracycline — the wonder antibiotic. At 73 years of age, he may well have helped more people to live than any other physician in the world.

TUESDAY — MAY 28

DIE when I may, I want it said by those who knew me best that I always plucked a thistle and planted a flower where I thought a flower would grow.

—*Abraham Lincoln*

WEDNESDAY — MAY 29

OUR Lord has written the promise of the Resurrection, not in books alone, but in every leaf in springtime.

—*Martin Luther*

THURSDAY — MAY 30

TO improve the golden moment of opportunity and catch the good that is within our reach, is the great art of life.

— *Samuel Johnson*

THE HERITAGE BOOK

TONIGHT we enjoyed some of Bruce's barbequed culinary delights for our dinner. The "chef's special" this evening was spicy hamburgers — chopped beef with spices and sauces, cooked to perfection and served on a soft kaiser roll. They were simply delicious!

I had assumed that the hamburger was a recent North American concoction, but Bruce corrected me; ancient Egyptians were the first to eat hamburger — in the form of raw ground beef.

The hamburger got its name from Hamburg, Germany. Merchants from that port city brought raw ground beef from the Baltic states and the meal became known in Europe as a native dish of Hamburg.

It was brought to the U.S. by German immigrants during the 1800s.

Louis Lassen first served broiled ground beef between two slices of bread in 1900 at Louie's Lunch in New Haven, Connecticut. It gained great popularity in 1903 at the Louisiana Purchase Exhibition.

Whatever the origin, the hamburger is a delicious dinner!

June

L OVE is patient, love is kind and is not jealous: love does not brag and is not arrogant, it does not act unbecomingly: it does not seek its own, is not provoked, does not take into account a wrong suffered, does not rejoice in unrighteousness, but rejoices with the truth; bears all things, believes all things, hopes all things, endures all things.

But now abide faith, hope and love, these three; but the greatest of these is love.

These words, taken from the 13th chapter of Corinthians, were spoken on our wedding day on this date, many years ago.

George and I had a wonderful marriage, and I remember him today with love and thanks.

THE HERITAGE BOOK

O UR Lord God, we thank you for all our blessings, for life and health, for laughter and fun, for all our powers of mind and body, for our home and the love of dear ones, for everything that is beautiful, good and true.

But above all we thank you for giving your Son to be our Saviour and Friend.

May we always find our true happiness in pleasing you and in helping others to know and to love you for Christ's sake.

Amen.

— Book of Alternative Services

MONDAY — JUNE 3

A ND what is so rare as a day in June?
Then, if ever, come perfect days;
Then Heaven tries earth if it be in tune,
And over it softly her warm ear lays;
Whether we look, or whether we listen,
We hear life murmur or see it glisten;
Every clod feels a stir of might,
An instinct within it that reaches and towers
And groping blindly above it for light,
Climbs to a soul in grass and flowers.

— James Russell Lowell

THE HERITAGE BOOK

MIX a little foolishness with your serious plans. It's lovely to be silly at the right moment.

— Horace

PART of the happiness of life consists not in fighting battles but in avoiding them. A masterly retreat is in itself a victory.

— Norman Vincent Peale

LIFE is mostly froth and bubble.
Two things stand like stone;
Kindness in another's trouble,
Courage in our own.

—Adam L. Gordon

THE HERITAGE BOOK

As my former readers know, I am a voracious reader. I have some old favourite books that I reread many times: *Anne of Green Gables, Tom Sawyer* and *Sunshine Sketches of a Little Town*, to name but a few.

As well, I enjoy reading books of all types — old and new. I offer you today others' thoughts on books.

A jolly good book whereon to look is better to me than gold.

—John Wilson

A good book is the best of friends, the same today and forever.

—Martin Tupper

A good book is the precious life-blood of a master spirit, embalmed and treasured up on purpose to a life beyond life.

— John Milton

A book that is shut is but a block.

—Thomas Fuller

There is no Frigate like a Book
To take us Lands away.

—Emily Dickinson

THE HERITAGE BOOK

I NEVER cease to be amazed by the advances in the field of science and medicine.

Nerve transplants are becoming more and more common. The world's first nerve transplant from one person to another was performed several years ago on a nine-year-old American boy who had damaged his sciatic nerve, which runs from the spine to the lower thigh, in a boating accident.

Using microsurgical techniques, the graft was built up like a telephone cable, from light thin strands, and connected the severed ends of the nerve. The graft acted as a scaffolding for regeneration of the boy's own new nerve tissue. Donor nerves grew along the graft at about two and a half centimetres per month and the boy's own nerve was restored in about two years.

Since that first graft, doctors have had success in many other cases of accidental nerve severance.

Perhaps this is the beginning of possible repairs of spinal cord injuries.

THE HERITAGE BOOK

TODAY was my birthday and I received the nicest gift that I could imagine. My sister Sarah arrived to give her good wishes in person. Imagine my surprise when I looked up to see her standing on our threshold! We were both quite giddy with delight for the rest of the afternoon.

There is no greater gift than a happy family.

SARAH and I had a leisurely day together. Today we visited with Ben and his wife Marie, and we strolled down memory lane, reliving our days as children on Canada's east coast. Marie enjoyed the stories immensely. She didn't know Ben until he was in his twenties, and the tales of our young brother's exploits kept her in stitches.

Later, Sarah and I took cups of tea to bed and chatted well into the night, as we often did as young girls. It was as if we were reluctant to waste the time that could be spent talking on anything as unimportant as sleep.

You know, a good friend is something to be greatly prized. A sister who is a best friend is a treasure whose value cannot be measured.

THE HERITAGE BOOK

TUESDAY — JUNE 11

SIMPLE and fresh and far from winter's close
emerging,
As if no artifice of fashion, business, politics
had ever been,
Forth from its sunny nook of shelter'd grass —
innocent, golden, calm as the dawn,
The spring's first dandelion shows its trustful
face.

—Walt Whitman

WEDNESDAY — JUNE 12

MAN'S greatest sin is not hatred, but
indifference to one's brothers.

—Mother Teresa

THURSDAY — JUNE 13

THERE is no accomplishment so easy to
acquire as politeness, and none more
profitable.

—George Bernard Shaw

THE HERITAGE BOOK

I BADE my sister Sarah a difficult goodbye at the airport today. We had a wonderful visit, but too brief. She has commitments at home, however, and felt that a week was as much time as she could be away.

I guess that as we advance in years, leave-taking is something that many of us find stressful. Neither Sarah nor I are young women and because of the distance between our homes, I harbour that secret fear that goes unspoken— "Will I see Sarah again?" It certainly makes for an embarrassing scene at the airport — two little old ladies hugging and weeping.

I really am grateful for the time that we shared and I shall continue to enjoy the memories that we created together.

TREAT your guests like family and your family like guests.

THE HERITAGE BOOK

O<small>N</small> this Father's Day, I present "Father":

4-year-old — My Daddy can do anything.

7-year-old — My Dad knows a whole lot.

9-year-old — My father doesn't quite know everything.

12-year-old — Oh well, fathers don't know everything.

14-year-old — Fathers! They're hopelessly old-fashioned.

21-year-old — Oh, that man is out of date! What did you expect?

25-year-old — He knows a little about it, but not much.

30-year-old — Must find out what Dad thinks about it.

35-year-old — A little patience, let's get Dad's ideas first.

50-year-old — What would Dad have thought about it?

60-year-old — My Dad knew literally everything.

65-year-old — I wish I could talk it over with Dad once more.

MONDAY — JUNE 17

YOU cannot box a sunset.
It is hard to wrap up snow.
There is no way to package
A lighted candle's glow.
Enjoy each lovely moment
As you walk along the way.
There is a bit of beauty
In every passing day.

—*Joyce Sandeen Johnson*

TUESDAY — JUNE 18

As the spring of this year sees its last few days I think of Henry Wordsworth Longfellow's wonderful words on this most beautiful time of renewal:

If spring came but once in a century, instead of once a year, or burst forth with the sound of an earthquake, and not in silence, what wonder and expectation there would be in all hearts to behold the miraculous change. But now the silent succession suggests nothing but necessity. To most men only the cessation of the miracle would be miraculous, and the perpetual exercise of God's power seems less wonderful than its withdrawal would be.

THE HERITAGE BOOK

M Y friend Lila and I have taken advantage of the fine weather to lengthen our daily walks. Our journeys have included the street that passes our local high school. As this is usually about the half-way point on our walk, we have often stopped to watch those students who were participating in the extra-curricular sports activities on the outdoor playing fields.

Lila most enjoyed the soccer games and on several occasions she became a very vocal fan, loudly cheering any particularly good plays made by "our" team.

I enjoyed watching the young men and women who were practising high-jumping. I found it fascinating to see the concentration and grace of form needed to soar over the bar. Often the bar would be higher than I could imagine anyone could jump and yet jump it they did.

I wonder if the sensation would be somewhat like flying?

Although the students are eagerly anticipating the coming vacation, there will be two old ladies wishing the school year would never end.

WE reach for perfection but we should pray that we do not get it. For if we do, to what can we then reach?

— *Bern Williams*

WHO drives the horses of the sun
Shall lord it but a day;
Better the lowly deed were done,
And kept the humble way.

The rust will find the sword of fame
The dust will hide the crown;
Aye, none shall nail so high his name
Time will not tear it down.

The happiest heart that ever beat
Was in some quiet breast
That found the common daylight sweet,
And left to Heaven the rest.

SHORT visits make long friends.

THE HERITAGE BOOK

ALMIGHTY God, we thank you for making the fruitful earth produce what is needed for life. Bless those who work in the field, give us favourable weather and grant that all may share the fruits of the earth, rejoicing in your goodness, through Jesus Christ our Lord.

—Book of Alternative Services

THE more a man finds his sources of pleasure in himself, the happier he will be.

—Arthur Schopenhauer

TO reach the port of Heaven we must sail sometimes with the wind and sometimes against it. But we must sail, and not drift nor lie at anchor.

—Oliver Wendell Holmes

THE HERITAGE BOOK

THIS is one of those little known facts that my son-in-law Bruce finds very fascinating. Did you know that a whisper can be heard for a distance of 162 feet in the cupola of St. Paul's cathedral in London? This cupola is known as the Whispering Gallery because of its curious echo. A slight whisper near the wall on one side of the gallery will be distinctly audible near the wall on the opposite side.

AT this time of year, many American visitors come to explore Canada's tourist areas.

Many years ago, an American friend visiting in Ontario was stopped for speeding. His explanation was captivating.

Charged with driving at 72 m.p.h., he explained that since the Canadian gallon was larger than the U.S. gallon, he thought that miles might be longer in Canada. To cover 60 Canadian miles in an hour he thought that his speedometer should read at least 70 miles per hour.

The policeman explained the error and waived the usual fine — "Welcome, guest."

THE HERITAGE BOOK

I GUESS it's a shame to have a factual memory.
After all, part of the charm of life is what
might have happened.

— *Morley Callaghan*

YOU can make more friends in two months
by becoming interested in other people
than you can in two years by trying to get
other people interested in you.

— *Dale Carnegie*

LORD temper with tranquility
Our manifold activity
That we may do our work for Thee
With very great simplicity.

— *Sixteenth century prayer*

July

A LTHOUGH this poem is titled "A Prayer for This House," I think that "Country" might be substituted for "House" to make an excellent thought for this 124th Canada Day.

May nothing evil cross this door,
And may ill fortune never pry
About these windows; may the roar
And rains go by.

Strengthened by faith, the rafters will
Withstand the battering of the storm.
This hearth, though all the world grow chill,
Will keep you warm.

Laughter shall drown the raucous shout
And, though the sheltering walls are thin,
May they be strong to keep hate out
And hold love in.

— *Louis Untermeyer*

THE HERITAGE BOOK

CONTENT makes poor men rich; discontent makes rich men poor.

—*Benjamin Franklin*

TONIGHT Marg, Bruce and I enjoyed a wonderful evening's entertainment. We attended a "mini-soccer" game in a nearby park to watch Jenny and Justin play their first league match. "Mini-soccer" means that a smaller field is used — about one half of a regular field — and the goals are smaller. The children involved are 5- and 6-year-olds, both boys and girls, and they are being taught the fundamentals of the game.

Some of the youngsters are very enthusiastic and they vigorously chase the ball up and down the field as fast as their little legs can carry them. Justin is very keen and I'm sure he ran miles during the game. Jenny prefers to choose a spot, usually where she and a friend can chat, and waits patiently until the ball comes to her. She then gives a hefty kick and carries on socializing. All in all it was a most lively and entertaining performance.

Thursday — July 4

THIS is a special day south of the border. Our American friends will proudly fly the patriotic display celebrating Independence Day and the birth of the United States of America.

President John F. Kennedy gave a stirring inaugural address in which he challenged Americans to "ask not what your country can do for you — ask what you can do for your country." It's a fitting challenge, I believe, on this "Glorious Fourth."

Friday — July 5

DURING these warm summer days and evenings, many campers and cottagers delight in using the canoe as a form of transportation or relaxation. It's interesting to note that in spite of technological advances, no one has been able to improve upon the design of the Indian canoe. The birch bark may be replaced by canvas or fibreglass, but the lines and model are just the same.

THE HERITAGE BOOK

My grandson Marshall is a lawyer and is interested in amusing or unusual stories from his profession, which Jake Frampton can always be counted on to provide. Today's visit was no exception.

Judge O.M. Martin, a full-blooded Mohawk Indian, was the first Native appointed to the bench in Canada.

One day he faced a man accused of stealing. The man pleaded guilty, and when his lengthy criminal record was produced, His Worship addressed him.

"You have a bad record here, sir."

"I was framed on all of them charges. The police got it in for me, I don't know why," he replied.

"But you pleaded guilty, sir," said Martin. "The accused will go to jail for three months."

As he was leaving, the prisoner muttered, "Jeez, imagine that! A white man like me doin' time 'cause a bloody redskin says so."

Everyone, including Martin, heard the remark. "Please face the bench," said His Worship to the accused.

"Me Big Chief here. So, paleface, you spend FOUR months in pokey instead of three for bad-mouth talk. You go now, paleface."

SUNDAY — JULY 7

JUDGE not, and ye shall not be judged: con-
demn not, and ye shall not be condemned:
forgive, and ye shall be forgiven.

— Luke 6:37

MONDAY — JULY 8

I'LL walk with gentle pace,
And choose the smoothest place,
And careful dip the oar,
And shun the winding shore,
And gently steer my boat
Where water-lilies float,
And cardinal flowers
Stand in their sylvan bowers.

— Henry David Thoreau

TUESDAY — JULY 9

SOME people are always grumbling that
roses have thorns; I am thankful that thorns
have roses.

— Alphonse Karr

THE HERITAGE BOOK

YESTERDAY was Justin's and Jenny's sixth birthday. The children enjoyed a party at home with their close friends yesterday afternoon, and then Phyllis and Bill held a family party tonight to commemorate the occasion.

As we ate our cake and ice cream with these two healthy and happy six-year-olds, it was difficult to remember that six years earlier they were tiny bird-like creatures in hospital incubators.

How lucky they were to be born in a country where medical advances allow such tiny babies not only to live, but to thrive and grow to be healthy children.

As I watched I thought how proud my husband George would have been of our two beautiful great-grandchildren.

THE ideals which have lighted my way, and time after time have given me new courage to face life cheerfully, have been kindness, beauty, and truth.

— *Albert Einstein*

FRIDAY — JULY 12

Music washes away from the soul the dust of everyday life.

— Berthold Auerbach

SATURDAY — JULY 13

My friends Muriel and Will stopped in to-day after visiting a friend at the hospital. When I asked after their friend's health, Will laughed and said, "He's getting better, that's for sure. He told us that two weeks ago when he would press the button to call a nurse, a half dozen nurses and any passing doctor would come to his bedside on the run. Now when he pushes the buzzer, they generally finish their coffee before strolling down to his room. 'That must mean I'm on the mend!'"

SUNDAY — JULY 14

Almighty God, you have made us for yourself, and our hearts are restless until they find their rest in you. May we find peace in your service, and in the world to come see you face to face, through Jesus Christ, our Lord.

Amen.

THE HERITAGE BOOK

IN families where both parents work, it can be difficult to provide care for their children during the long summer break from school.

Recently Marg and I attended a seminar that discussed this topic and offered some practical solutions for parents facing this dilemma.

One excellent idea was to take advantage of 14- or 15-year-old students who are off school for the summer, but are too young to be hired as full-time workers. These young people are often anxious to earn some money, and careful choosing will usually find a conscientious companion.

Many areas offer "day camps." They operate under the guidance of the municipal Parks and Recreation department, and they offer a variety of activities: arts and crafts, sports, special event trips, and a host of other activities enjoyed by children.

Live-in camps are an alternative, albeit an expensive choice.

Some parents may choose to take advantage of interested retirees in their area. Often these people could well use a supplement to their fixed incomes, and many happy relationships can result.

TUESDAY — JULY 16

To go against the dominant thinking of your friends, of most of the people you see every day, is perhaps the most difficult act of heroism you can perform.

WEDNESDAY — JULY 17

How many of us, reading these words by Robert Louis Stevenson, remember the joy of a swing ride in summer?

How do you like to go up in a swing,
Up in the air so blue?
Oh, I do think it the pleasantest thing
Ever a child can do!

Up in the air and over the wall,
Till I can see so wide,
Rivers and trees and cattle and all
Over the countryside —

Till I look down on the garden green,
Down on the roof so brown —
Up in the air I go flying again,
Up in the air and down!

THURSDAY — JULY 18

WE are all of us fellow passengers on the same planet and we are all of us equally responsible for the happiness and the well-being of the world in which we happen to live.

— *Hendrick Willem Van Loon*

FRIDAY — JULY 19

I CAN see how it might be possible for a man to look down upon the earth and be an atheist, but I cannot conceive how he could look up into the heavens and say there is no God.

— *Abraham Lincoln*

SATURDAY — JULY 20

HAPPINESS in this world, when it comes, comes incidentally. Make it the object of pursuit, and it is never attained.

— *Nathaniel Hawthorne*

THE HERITAGE BOOK

Love your enemies, do good to those who hate you. Bless those who curse you, pray for those who spitefully treat you. Treat others as you would like them to treat you.

— *Luke 6:28-29:31*

Song

How sweet I roam'd from field to field
and tasted all the summer's pride,
'Till I the prince of love beheld,
Who in the sunny beams did glide!

He shew'd me lilies for my hair,
And blushing roses for my brow;
He led me through his gardens fair,
Where all his golden pleasures grow.

He loves to sit and hear me sing,
Then, laughing, sports and plays with me;
Then stretches out my golden wing,
And mocks my loss of liberty.

— *William Blake*

THE HERITAGE BOOK

THIS is Marg and Bruce's wedding anniversary. To celebrate the occasion, I offer a portion of Helen Steiner Rice's poem, "The Magic Of Love."

Love is like magic
And it always will be,
For love still remains
Life's sweet mystery!

Love works in ways
That are wondrous and strange
And there's nothing in life
That love cannot change!

Love can transform
The most commonplace
Into beauty and splendor
And sweetness and grace!

Love is unselfish,
Understanding and kind,
For it sees with its heart
And not with its mind!

WEDNESDAY — JULY 24

WITH the intense heat that we have had in recent weeks, sleeping has been quite difficult. Lila McGuiness and I spent some time today discussing methods of cooling ourselves and, we hope, of sleeping better during heat waves.

Something that often helps me is a warm bath. Coming out of a warm bath seems to make the air seem just a little cooler, at least for a short time.

Lila finds that if she places cool washcloths over her eyes and on the inside of both wrists she feels much more comfortable. Frosty iced tea sipped at bedtime was also a help for her.

Sleeping on a screened porch or in a basement room is another recommended "cooler."

Probably the best idea is to remember back to those frigid days of winter when we longed for the heat of summer — and enjoy it.

THURSDAY — JULY 25

EVERY man has three characters — that which he exhibits, that which he has, and that which he thinks he has.

—Alphonse Karr

THE HERITAGE BOOK

JANE Taylor wrote these lines about one of my favourite summer flowers, the violet.

Down in a green and shady bed
A modest violet grew;
Its stalk was bent, it hung its head,
As if to hide from view.

And yet it was a lovely flower
Its colour bright and fair;
It might have graced a rosy bower,
Instead of hiding there.

Yet there it was content to bloom
In modest tints arrayed;
And there diffused a sweet perfume,
Within the silent shade.

Then let me to the valley go,
This pretty flower to see,
That I may also learn to grow
In sweet humility.

SELF-CONFIDENCE is the ability to endure misfortune without looking for someone to blame.

THE HERITAGE BOOK

JOYFUL, Joyful, we adore thee
God of glory, Lord of love
Hearts unfold like flowers before thee
Opening to the sun above.
Melt the clouds of sin and sadness
Drive the dark of doubt away —
Giver of immortal gladness,
Fill us with the light of day.
— *Henry Van Dyke*

FEW things help an individual more than to
place responsibility upon him, and to let
him know that you trust him.
— *Booker T. Washington*

MATURITY is when you realize how much
you thought you knew, but didn't.

THE HERITAGE BOOK

WHEN I think of summer camp, I envision children sleeping in tents amid tall pine trees, swimming in cool lake water, or sailing and canoeing. So I laughed when I read a letter from my friend Emily telling me about a summer "camp" in Palm Beach, Florida called the "Money Management Camp" for kids.

The camp is based in The Breakers Hotel, an exclusive retreat used by the wealthy in winter months. The children come from all over the United States and Canada to learn the rudiments of money management. These children come from wealthy families, and the parents want to be sure that the children, who are going to have money, know how to manage it.

The childrens' opinions of the camp range from "It's boring — extremely boring!" to "I really like it; it's interesting to learn about investments."

To be honest with you, a tent in the woods sounds infinitely more appealing to me.

August

The Cloud

I BRING fresh showers for the thirsting flowers,
From the seas and the streams;
I bear light shade for the leaves when laid
In their noonday dreams.
From my wings are shaken the dews that
   waken
The sweet buds every one,
When rocked to rest on their mother's breast,
As she dances about the sun.
I wield the flail of the lashing hail,
And whiten the green plains under,
And then again I dissolve it in rain,
And laugh as I pass in thunder.

                              — *Percy Bysshe Shelley*

THE HERITAGE BOOK

THE two things that a person tends to keep with them throughout life are the memory of their mother and the music they grew up on.

— *Richard C. Miller*

THE Ontario city of St. Catharines is known as "The Garden City." Just exactly when it picked up this name is not known, but a best guess would seem to be around 1865.

In a most interesting article by Gail Benjafield, a resident of the city and local historian, I learned that the City Directory of 1874 lauded the nurseries as "the most extensive in the Dominion, equalling in variety the most celebrated and largest in Europe or America."

Mrs. Benjafield explains that the city, nestled safely under the escarpment, has climates and soils that lend themselves perfectly to the growing of a variety of flowers, fruits and vegetables.

Market Square Days are Tuesday, Thursday and Saturday, and this beautiful city is well worth a summer visit.

THE HERITAGE BOOK

GOD, our creator and sustainer, accept all we offer you this day, and feed us continually with that bread which satisfies all hunger, Your Son, our Saviour, Jesus Christ.

Amen.

How happy I am to be back once again in beautiful Muskoka. Each year I eagerly anticipate my visit with my dear friend Eleanor in this beautiful area of Ontario.

This year's trip up was slightly different because I came by bus. Usually Marg and Bruce drive me, but because of other commitments, they were unable to do so.

What a delightful trip I had! I boarded the bus in Toronto and was seated beside a young lad of about ten. In our ensuing conversation I found out that Chris was heading to Muskoka to visit with his grandparents who have a cottage on Lake Rosseau. Chris was a very polite and charming travel companion and I'm sure his grandparents will greatly enjoy his company.

THE HERITAGE BOOK

IT must be the northern air that induces such deep sleep. I usually rise with the birds, but this morning I didn't stir until I heard the toot of the *Segwun* steamship whistle as it passed by the end of Eleanor's dock. I was startled, to say the least, to realize that it was already after 9 a.m.

I hurried to the front porch to watch the *Segwun* sail out of sight. I never tire of watching this magnificent old boat. Built in 1887, it ran as one of the fleet of steamships that carried passengers, cargo and mail around the Muskoka Lakes to various resorts.

As roads were built and land travel became more popular, the steamships became obsolete.

The *Segwun* sat in drydock for many years until, in 1967, the town of Gravenhurst undertook its refurbishing as a centennial project.

The boat now runs daily cruises on the lakes and, as well, is often rented for private parties such as weddings.

It is a wonderful piece of history and interesting to people of all ages.

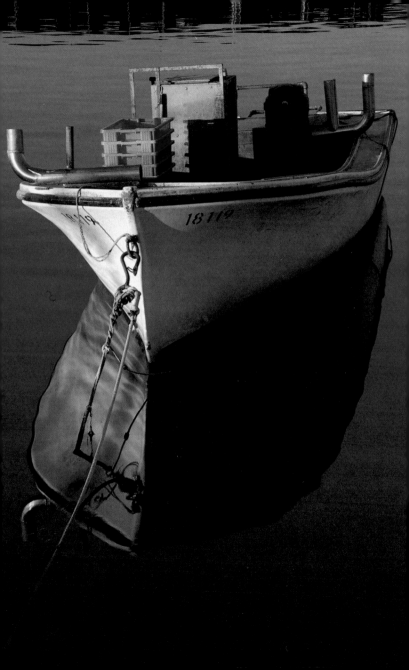

WEDNESDAY — AUGUST 7

"CURIOSITY," Arnold Edinborough once concluded, "is the very basis of education; and if you tell me that curiosity killed the cat, I say the cat died nobly."

THURSDAY — AUGUST 8

THIS evening as we sat on the front porch, an owl sat hooting in a nearby tree. As I listened I was reminded of Henry David Thoreau who sat alone at Walden Pond so many summers ago listening to just such an owl.

"I was also serenaded by a hooting owl. I rejoice that there are owls. Let them do the idiotic and maniacal hooting for men. It is a sound admirably suited to swamps and twilight woods which no day illustrates, suggesting a vast and undeveloped nature which men have not recognized. They represent the stark twilight and unsatisfied thoughts which all have."

FRIDAY — AUGUST 9

THY beauty haunts me heart and soul,
O thou fair moon, so close and bright;
Thy beauty makes me like the child,
That cries aloud to own thy light:
The little child that lifts each arm,
To press thee to her bosom warm.

Though there are birds that sing this night
With thy white beams across their throats,
Let my deep silence speak for me
More than for them their sweetest notes:
Who worships thee till music fails
Is greater than thy nightengales.

— W.H. Davies

SATURDAY — AUGUST 10

THE imagination gallops but judgement
goes on foot.

SUNDAY — AUGUST 11

"I AM the living bread which came down
from heaven," said Jesus. "Anyone who
eats this bread will live forever."

— John 6:51

THE HERITAGE BOOK

MONDAY — AUGUST 12

FROM the unreal — lead me to the real,
From darkness — lead me to light,
From death — lead me to immortality.
                    — *Brihadaranyaka Upanishad*

TUESDAY — AUGUST 13

SAMUEL Johnson once noted that the two most engaging powers of an author are that new things are made familiar and familiar things are made new.

WEDNESDAY — AUGUST 14

AFTER many years of "wash and wear" clothes, the new designer-label clothing seems to require very special treatment.

It was with peals of laughter that Eleanor read to me the label on a pair of pants, obviously designed for a young person.

FOR BEST RESULTS: Machine wash, cold, separately — gentle cycle only. Do not bleach. Lay flat to dry. Warm iron.

FOR NOT SO GOOD RESULTS: Drag behind car through puddles and blow-dry on roof rack.

THE HERITAGE BOOK

I HOLD him dearest who aspires
To kindle in my heart the fires
Of best desires.

I hold the man of all most dear
Who, when I stumble, draweth near
With word of cheer.

I hold that man of best interests
Who giveth me not paltry pence,
But confidence.

For there are men who quick caress
Will give to laurel — crowned success —
To nothing less.

But, oh, how dearer far are they
Who help me on the upward way
When skies are grey.

If so it be that I attain
The mountain peak, and leave the plain
And paths of pain,

My prayers shall first be upward sent
For those dear friends of mine who lent
Encouragement.

— Douglas Malloch

Watching the young people swimming to-day, I was reminded of a great Canadian Olympic swimmer, Victor Davis.

Born in Guelph, Ontario in 1964, he began swimming at an early age. It became clear that as well a wonderful talent for the sport, he had that indefinable something that sets champions above the rest.

Victor came into prominence in Brisbane, Australia when, in a fit of anger at his team's disqualification, he kicked a chair in the presence of H.R.H. Queen Elizabeth. This breach of etiquette just showed the determination and the intense desire to win that was his nature. He deplored mediocrity.

In 1988 he set a record on his leg of the 4 x 100 medley relay, pushing his team to the silver medal at the Olympics in Seoul, Korea. Victor died in a tragic car accident in 1989, but even in death he lives on, his parents having donated his organs for transplant.

He lived by his motto, "Only those who dare truly live," and he will be remembered as a true Canadian champion.

SATURDAY — AUGUST 17

THERE is a beautiful Indian apologue which says: A man once said to a lump of clay, "What art thou?" The reply was, "I am but a lump of clay, but I was placed beside a rose and I caught its fragrance."

— *William Morley Punshon*

SUNDAY — AUGUST 18

Now therefore keep thy sorrow to thyself, and bear with a good courage that which hath befallen thee.

— *The Apocrypha*

MONDAY — AUGUST 19

To be happy at home is the ultimate aim of all ambition; the end to which every enterprise and labour tends, and of which every desire prompts the prosecution.

— *Samuel Johnson*

THE HERITAGE BOOK

FOR some years now my son-in-law Bruce has been losing his hair. Unlike many men who go to great lengths to disguise the fact that they are going bald, Bruce has never been particularly disturbed about this happening. As he said, "I had only to look at my father, grandfather and brothers to realize that I was not likely to keep my hair for any great length of time."

In fact, Bruce finds the subject of baldness quite interesting. Here are some facts he has learned:

One out of every five men begins to go bald right after puberty and is completely bald by age 30. This is not a new problem. Mexican cave paintings show that prehistoric men lost their hair, too. The earliest recorded baldness remedy dates back to 4000 B.C., when the mother of King Chata of Egypt recommended rubbing the bald head vigorously with a mixture of ground-up dog's paws, dates, and asses' hooves, cooked in oil!

According to the founder of "Bald-Headed Men of America," John T. Capps III of Morehead City, North Carolina, "The good Lord created only a few perfect heads — the rest He had to cover with hair!"

THE HERITAGE BOOK

KIND hearts are the gardens,
Kind thoughts are the roots,
Kind words are the flowers,
Kind deeds are the fruits.

Take care of the gardens,
And keep them from the weeds.
Fill, fill them with flowers,
Kind words and kind deeds.

— Henry Wadsworth Longfellow

MY friend Emily, who winters in Florida, keeps in touch by mail with her many southern friends during her summers in Philadelphia. One of her best friends recently moved into a church-affiliated senior-citizens' apartment complex in Winter Park in Florida.

The meals there are served cafeteria style with two lines: one for those in wheel-chairs and walkers, and the other for those without handicaps.

"I had such a laugh, Emily," wrote her friend, "when I heard what the other residents called the lines — 'Cane' and 'Able.'"

THE HERITAGE BOOK

THE test of good manners is to be able to put up pleasantly with bad ones.

SITTING outside under the northern lights to-night brought to mind a night such as this many years ago.

Back in the mid-'50s, we spent our summers living in an old log house that had been built in the mid-1800s. We worked long and hard, as a family, restoring this lovely place to its earlier grandeur.

One evening after a long day's work, we enjoyed a late supper of corn boiled on the barbeque pit down by the lake.

As the sun set and the stars came out, we sat quietly enjoying the beautiful evening. Gradually the northern sky came alive with flashing beams of light — bluish silver at first, and then, as they gained strength and power, in a multitude of colours. It seemed as if we could hear, as well as see, them.

When we finally went into the house we felt as though we had seen a brief glimpse into the beauty of eternity.

SUNDAY — AUGUST 25

MAY God be merciful to us and bless us. Show the light of his countenance and come to us. Let your way be known upon earth, your saving health among all nations. Let the people praise you, O God. Let all thy people praise you.

— Psalm 67:1-3

MONDAY — AUGUST 26

ANY of you who have had a fire in your home will identify with the panic-stricken man who recently called our local fire station.

"My house is on fire!" he yelled at the man receiving the call.

"How do we get there?" asked the fireman.

"Well, don't you have your red truck anymore?" shouted the poor man in alarm.

TUESDAY — AUGUST 27

CHARACTER is much easier kept than recovered.

— Thomas Paine

WEDNESDAY — AUGUST 28

My heart leaps up when I behold a rainbow
in the sky:
So was it when my life began;
So is it now I am a man;
So be it when I shall grow old,
Or let me die!
The Child is father of the Man;
And I could wish my days to be
Bound each to each by natural piety.
                              — *William Wordsworth*

THURSDAY — AUGUST 29

Tonight there was a chill in the evening air as I took my walk, and the light has been fading a little earlier each evening. I greet with mixed emotions these signals of the end of summer. Autumn, with its glorious colours and bountiful harvests, is a magnificent time of the year. But I shall miss the long, warm and lazy days of summer.

THE HERITAGE BOOK

THIS is the last long weekend of the summer and many people will use this time for a last trip north to the cottage. Years ago, before the popularity of organized sport, numerous families would use the cottage for many weekends into the fall. This doesn't seem to happen anymore.

Just this week our local newspaper announced that the "Rep." hockey tryouts would begin this weekend. Any boys who wish to play for these high-calibre hockey teams this winter must attend the tryouts tomorrow and Sunday.

Without being critical of the many volunteers who put so much time and effort into minor hockey, would the entire season be ruined if these young lads and their families were given this one last weekend of the summer to enjoy in summer activities? I think not.

THE best thing about the future is that it comes one day at a time.

— *Abraham Lincoln*

September

A LMIGHTY God, your son Jesus Christ digni-
fied our labour by sharing our toil. Be
with your people wherever they work. Make
those who carry on the industries and com-
merce of this land responsive to your will, and
to all of us give pride in what we do and a just
return for our labour, through your son Jesus
Christ.

Amen.

N o man is born into the world, whose work
is not born with him; there is always
work, and tools to work withal, for those who
will: and blessed are the horny hands of toil!
— *James Russell Lowell*

TUESDAY — SEPTEMBER 3

IN most areas, today is the day that children return to the "halls of learning."

Marg and I enjoyed our tea on the porch this morning, the better to watch the youngsters in our area return to meet their old friends and new teachers. Many of the children skipped up our walkway to say hello on their way.

I enjoy very much living in an area where there are a number of children. I like their enthusiasm for life, their noise, their happy spirits. I hope I will always have these youngsters near me to keep me young in spirit.

WEDNESDAY — SEPTEMBER 4

SIR Frederick Banting, the co-discoverer of insulin, was an ardent amateur painter who sometimes sketched with A.Y. Jackson and other members of the "Group of Seven." Thoreau McDonald (son of the Group's J.E.H. McDonald, and himself a well-known illustrator) was not one of the admirers of Banting's artistic efforts. Hearing of Banting's death in a 1941 plane crash, he wrote to a friend, "Too bad, but at least he won't do any more painting."

THE HERITAGE BOOK

S HE'S starting off to school today
And oh, she seems so small,
A little bit of loveliness
Just forty inches tall.
She has so very much to learn,
Like sitting still and such,
She's always been so much alive —
Do use a gentle touch.

She'll be your little girl today
And oh, my heart does ache,
The afternoons will be so long
For her to stay awake.
She's really not a naughty child
Although she loves to tease,
You'll find her little mind alert —
So teach her gently, please.

She's starting off to school today,
And because I love her so,
Like all the mothers in the world
I hate to see her go.
Although I'm sure you understand
Such little ones as these,
Because she's all my hopes and dreams
Do teach her gently, please.

— *Garnett Ann Schultz*

THE HERITAGE BOOK

Jake Frampton stopped by for dinner this evening, and he came bearing a beautiful floral arrangement. Jake knows how much I enjoy flowers and he often drops arrangements off for me for no particular occasion.

What I like most about Jake's arrangements is that he never asks the florist to choose the flowers. He marches right into their storage room and chooses the flowers that he wants the florist to arrange. Although he doesn't do the actual arrangement himself, the blooms he selects exhibit his wonderful sense of colour and balance, and the resulting arrangements are spectacular.

When I asked about this talent, he laughed it off, saying, "I look at flowers the way I look at books. If they are different sizes and colours I know they will look good together."

However he does it, I appreciate his thoughtfulness immensely. Not everyone is blessed with such a kind friend and I truly am thankful for such a one as Jake.

THE HERITAGE BOOK

THERE is only a slight difference between keeping your chin up and sticking your neck out, but it's worth knowing.

WE sang this hymn, one of my favourites, at church today.

Abide with me, fast falls the eventide;
The darkness deepens; Lord with me abide:
When other helpers fail, and comforts flee,
Help of the helpless, oh, abide with me!

I need Thy presence every passing hour:
What but Thy grace can foil the tempter's
    power?
Who like Thyself my guide and stay can be?
Through cloud and sunshine, oh, abide with
    me!

Hold then Thy cross before my closing eyes;
Shine through the gloom, and point me to the
    skies:
Heaven's morning breaks, and earth's vain
    shadows flee —
In life and death, O Lord, abide with me!
                                        — *Henry F. Lyte*

THE HERITAGE BOOK

THREE rules of life were given me some years ago. I pass them on for I have found them practical. The first is "Go," the second is "Keep going," and the third is "Help someone else to go."

I HEAR the blackbird in the corn,
The locust in the haying:
And, like the fabled hunters horn,
Old tunes my heart is playing.
— *John Greenleaf Whittier*

THE HERITAGE BOOK

THAT old adage "Never judge a book by its cover" proved itself true again today.

Marg and I had decided to spend the day in downtown Toronto doing some shopping. We rode the Go train and then the subway up Yonge St. to the Eaton's Centre. At the Eaton's Centre we decided to separate for a few hours — Marg had some special items to find and I preferred a more leisurely stroll through this beautiful mall. We agreed to meet at a specified time and place.

I enjoyed my wanderings — there are so many interesting stores to browse through.

As I stopped to look in the window of a gift shop, a young man grasped my arm and said, "Excuse me." He was one of three men whose appearance certainly didn't inspire confidence. They had long hair, torn jeans and an extremely scruffy appearance. As I was about to yell for help the man said, "I think you dropped this," and he returned my wallet — intact — which had somehow fallen from my purse.

A BIG-LEAGUE umpire once remarked that he could never understand how crowds in the stands, hundreds of feet from home plate, could see better, and judge balls and strikes more accurately, than he, when he was only a few feet away.

T HERE'S a mighty big difference between good, sound reasons and reasons that sound good.

E DUCATION can't make us all leaders, but it can teach us which leader to follow.

SUNDAY — SEPTEMBER 15

S ING to the Lord of Harvest,
Sing songs of love and praise,
With joyful hearts and voices
Your hallelujahs raise.
By him the rolling seasons,
In fruitful order move
Sing to the Lord of Harvest
A joyful song of love.
— *John Samuel Bewley Monpell*

MONDAY — SEPTEMBER 16

M ONEY and time are the heaviest burdens of life, and the unhappiest of all mortals are those who have more of either than they know how to use.

TUESDAY — SEPTEMBER 17

T HE best help is not to bear the troubles of others for them, but to inspire them with courage and energy to bear their burdens for themselves and meet the difficulties of life bravely.
— *John Lubbock*

THE HERITAGE BOOK

ALTHOUGH no one appreciates today's grocery stores with their fresh merchandise any more than I do, there is something I really miss.

I miss the old-time milkman, and breadman. How I looked forward each day to their visits, and to the chance to choose from their loaded trucks each item that I needed (or longed for).

My favourite was the milk in the quart bottle — the top third was filled with a thick cream that we used in our coffee or on the girls' cereal. That cream was so thick and rich it always seemed as if the cow must have given it that very day.

The bread truck, in addition to its fresh bread, usually carried sweet buns and jelly rolls that were special favourites of my husband George.

What I most enjoyed, however, was the chance to chat with these men who delivered. We came to know their families, as well as many of their hopes and interests.

THE HERITAGE BOOK

As we walked through our neighbourhood today, I couldn't help but notice how quickly some of our trees are changing colour. This is a truly beautiful time of year and "Indian Summer" by Ruby Brown captures the essence of this lovely time.

Come, let me take your hand
To walk with you where azure smoke
Holds autumn in an acorn cup,
And paints the elm, the ash, and oak.

Where golden feathered grenadiers
Guard well the mottled zigzag fence;
And asters wear a purple veil,
Wide eyes searching for the prince.

Wait! He comes, the rusty flute
Of crows prelude his silent tread;
The hickory dons his golden coat
To stand aloof where moss is spread.

Tiptoe now . . . there, you see?
His scarlet banners on the hill,
Hear the drums now rolling free. . . .
He comes this way, be still, be still.

FRIDAY — SEPTEMBER 20

MORALE is when your hands and feet keep working although your head says it can't be done.

SATURDAY — SEPTEMBER 21

ALTHOUGH the autumnal equinox sometimes plays games with the calendar, and autumn sneaks in a day late or a day early, this is the usual day for welcoming the new season.

Our family chose a very pleasant way to welcome the fall. We had a family get-together at my grandson Marshall and his wife Jamie's new home.

This young couple have spent considerable time searching for a house that they both liked (as well as one that suited their budget).

They were able to find an old home near the village of Limehouse. Although it needs extensive renovation and redecorating, it is structurally sound and has a beautiful property.

During dinner, Marshall announced that he and Jamie had yet another reason to be joyous. They plan to make me a great-grandmother in the new year. What a wonderful way to welcome autumn.

SUNDAY — SEPTEMBER 22

ALMIGHTY God, you have created the heavens and the earth and ourselves in your image. Teach us to discern your hand in all your works and to serve you with reverence and thanksgiving.

Amen.

MONDAY — SEPTEMBER 23

THE tree which moves some to tears of joy is in the eyes of others only a green thing that stands in the way.

— *William Blake*

TUESDAY — SEPTEMBER 24

A TEACHER who can arouse a feeling for one single good action, for one single good poem, accomplishes more than he who fills our memory with rows on rows of natural objects, classified with name and form.

— *Johann Wolfgang von Goethe*

THE HERITAGE BOOK

THIS is the season of country fairs and village suppers. We watch with interest our magazines and rural newspapers to learn where and when we might be able to attend these fun affairs.

The good church folk who prepare these suppers seem to know that the brisk fall air renders enormous appetites and they cook accordingly.

At the supper in the Anglican church in our area, the tables were laden with platters of hot ham, whole turkeys, dishes of mashed potatoes, beans, carrots, corn, sliced tomatoes and for dessert, hot apple or peach pies with cream.

One of the most enjoyable aspects of these suppers is that we get to meet many people who are visitors from other areas of our province. Often people will drive many miles to enjoy the good food and fine fellowship that these dinners provide.

One word of caution — too many of these superb dinners can make for a long winter of dieting.

THE HERITAGE BOOK

GRANT that these autumn days may be our harvest season: that our lives may reap the fruits of a well-spent year.

— *Edwin Osgood Grover*

THIS is the time of year when three major sports seasons overlap. Baseball, football and hockey are being played in stadiums and arenas all over North America. For those of us who are fans, the weekend's television sports fare is a delight. For the less enthusiastic, it is a time to rake, clean or do other fall chores in preparation for the winter to come.

I had a good laugh from my neighbour, Bill, today.

"You know," he said, "It isn't that I am such a great sports fan, Edna, but Denise never wants to ask me to rake or do the other household chores while a sportscast is on, so I find I can learn to enjoy football, baseball, or any other sport!"

In fact, Bill was kidding. No one helps out around the house more than he does.

SATURDAY — SEPTEMBER 28

THE oldest short words — yes and no — are those which require the most thought.

— *Pythagoras*

SUNDAY — SEPTEMBER 29

AND God shall wipe away all tears from their eyes; and there shall be no more death, neither sorrow, nor crying, neither shall there be any more pain: for the former things are passed away.

— *Revelation 21:4*

MONDAY — SEPTEMBER 30

IN his book, Duke Ellington gave this moving tribute to Louis Armstrong: "He was born poor, died rich, and never hurt anyone on the way."

October

IT'S autumn in the country now,
The leaves are red and gold,
And beauty lies in flaming guise
On oak trees staunch and old.
The frost has blighted everything
That in the garden grew,
But chestnuts brown are falling down,
And autumn skies are blue.

It's autumn in the country now,
It's autumn in the town.
October trips with scarlet lips,
In blue and amber gown!
The cornfields soon will lie knee-deep
In snow's white mystery,
But autumn's in the country now,
Right where I long to be!

— *Anne Campbell*

THE HERITAGE BOOK

O N this day in 1869, Mohandas Gandhi, better known as Mahatma Gandhi, was born in India.

He was a great proponent of civil disobedience through non-violent resistance. These were the tactics that he used to lead his country to independence from British rule.

Perhaps the most important lesson that was taught by Gandhi was that if you speak peacefully and make sense, people will listen and will act on what you say.

It is a lesson that applies to all generations.

M ARG and I went to our local high school football game today.

Such fond memories are evoked when I am at these games. My husband George and I would often enjoy the games when the young men of our parish were involved.

George would say, "Edna, if these young men are involved in running and tackling and putting all of their hearts and efforts into the game, they will never have the time (or the energy) to get into trouble."

FRIDAY — OCTOBER 4

SUCCESS comes to the person who does today what you were thinking of doing tomorrow.

SATURDAY — OCTOBER 5

THERE are two great truths provided by education:
Before graduation — "I think, therefore I am."
After graduation — "I work, therefore I eat."

SUNDAY — OCTOBER 6

FOR the beauty of the earth,
For the glory of the skies,
For the love which from our birth
Over and around us lies,
Lord of all to thee we raise
This our grateful psalm of praise.

— *F.S. Pierpoint*

THE HERITAGE BOOK

Monday — October 7

Nᴇᴡ opinions are always suspected and usually opposed, without any other reason but because they are not already common.
— *John Locke*

Tuesday — October 8

Tʜɪs is the time of year when students are beginning their essays and projects. My friend Marcia, who works and writes in Boston, recently received a letter from a young student in her area.

The letter read, "I have chosen you as my favourite author. Please write me immediately in not less than 300 words and tell me why."

Wednesday — October 9

Tʜᴇʀᴇ is no future in any job. The future lies in the man who holds the job.
— *Dr. George Crane*

THE HERITAGE BOOK

THE Macmillan Dictionary gives this definition of the word conscience as "mental or emotional faculty that prompts one to do right and by which right and wrong are distinguished, especially with regard to one's own behaviour or motives."

Many people have contemplated the conscience, and I offer to you today a few of their ideas.

A peace above all earthly dignities,
A still and quiet conscience.
> — *Wolsey from Shakespeare's*
> King Henry VIII

This conscience does make cowards of us all.
> — *Hamlet from Shakespeare's* Hamlet

To sit alone with my conscience will be judgement enough for me.
> — *Charles William Stubbs*

Conscience is the guardian in the individual of the rules which the community has evolved for its own preservation.
> — *William Somerset Maugham*

THE HERITAGE BOOK

THIS is the beginning of the Thanksgiving holiday weekend in Canada. Phyllis's friend Christie, a teacher, asked the children in her class to write down what they were thankful for. I enjoyed their answers very much.

"I am thankful for my mom and dad."

"I am thankful that I always have enough to eat."

"I am thankful that my dog Kokomo loves me."

"I am thankful that both of my Grandmas are still alive even though they're *really* old."

"I am thankful that I have friends."

THE art of medicine consists of amusing the patient while nature cures the disease.
— *Voltaire*

SUNDAY — OCTOBER 13

N ow thank we all our God,
With heart and hands and voices,
Who wondrous things hath done,
In whom His world rejoices;
Who from our mother's arms
Hath blessed us on our way
With countless gifts of love,
And still is ours today.

— *Rev. Martin Winkworth*

MONDAY — OCTOBER 14
Canadian Thanksgiving Day

O N this day I was remembering a Thanksgiving from many years ago. George and I were living in a farming parish, and on Thanksgiving Day one of the homes in our area caught fire and burned to the ground, taking with it all of the family's worldly possessions. George and I hurried over to lend what help and support we could and when we arrived, the farmer, his wife and children were viewing the devastation. I will never forget the father's words: "Did we lose everything? No, we saved what was really important. Our family is all here safely together. This is a thankful day for us."

THE HERITAGE BOOK

OCTOBER is truly a beautiful month. The colours are at their peak and the days are not yet cool enough to be uncomfortable.

How I enjoy walking at this time of year. The vibrant colours really lift the spirits. As Lila and I strolled through the park today I was reminded of the poem "The Gifts of Autumn," by Catherine Donnelly.

Autumn came to visit me,
And as she hurried on,
She tripped and spilled her treasures
All over my front lawn.

Golden leaves and ruby ones
Of deepest jewel shades,
Gathered from her wanderings
Over valleys, hills and glades.

When I saw Autumn's treasures there
In brilliant disarray,
I quickly stooped and picked them up
And cherished them all day.

WEDNESDAY — OCTOBER 16

YOU can accurately gauge the worth of a young man by the attitude he has toward an old man.

— *Arnot L. Sheppard Jr.*

THURSDAY — OCTOBER 17

HOW inoffensive it is when a man repeats himself when he's saying nice things about you.

FRIDAY — OCTOBER 18

ALWAYS acknowledge a fault frankly. This will throw those in authority off their guard and give you the opportunity to commit more.

— *Mark Twain*

THE HERITAGE BOOK

THIS Saturday is "Fall Fair" in our area. I do so enjoy these special days in our town.

A part of the fair that impresses me immensely is the display of local school children's handiwork. Pieces of artwork, cooking, craftwork or storywriting are displayed and judged — each one winning a ribbon of merit, and many winning first-place ribbons in varying categories.

The talent displayed by some of these children is truly awe-inspiring. One particularly fine piece of artwork was a pencil sketch of a young girl wearing a Victorian-looking dress and sitting on a wicker settee. The attention to detail was magnificent; the girl in the picture looked as if she could rise and walk off the page. The artist was a young girl of 15 and I hope that she realizes what a wonderful talent she has. Better yet, I hope that someone else recognizes her talent and encourages her to develop what appears to be a tremendous potential.

It was a most enjoyable day!

THOU visitest the earth and blessest it: thou makest it very plenteous. The river of God is full of water: thou preparest their corn, for so thou providest for the earth. Thou crownest the year with thy goodness: and thy clouds drop fatness.

— *Psalm 65: 9-10*

COME, friend, my fire is burning bright,
A fire's no longer out of place,
How clear it glows! (there's frost tonight)
It looks white winter in the face.
— *Thomas Constable*

LIVING from pay day to pay day used to be considered a disgrace. Now it's an accomplishment.

THE HERITAGE BOOK

A SINGER whose music I admire is Julio Iglesias. Not until recently did I learn the story of how this man came to be in the field of music.

Julio Iglesias was a professional soccer player in Madrid, Spain, when a car accident ended his career, leaving him paralyzed for a year and a half. A nurse, working in the hospital where he was confined, bought Iglesias a guitar to help pass the long hours.

Although he had no prior musical training or aspirations, he soon became a tremendous success in pop music.

The accident that seemed at the time to have destroyed a man's career was merely a door-opener for an even greater success.

THERE'S a simple do-it-yourself face-lift that's sure to improve your looks; it's called a smile.

FRIDAY — OCTOBER 25

THE night will never stay,
The night will still go by,
Though with a million stars
You pin it to the sky;
Thou you bind it with the blowing wind
And buckle it with the moon,
The night will slip away
Like sorrow or a tune.

— Eleanor Farjeon

SATURDAY — OCTOBER 26

THIS was a busy but gratifying day. It was the day that we canned our many fruits and vegetables to see us through the long winter.

Although times have changed, this is one job that seems to have stayed constant over the many years. I can remember as a child all of our family gathering in the large kitchen to peel, pare, chop, boil and jar. Today was the same — there were merely different generations working together.

Tomatoes were so abundant this year that we were able to make chili sauce, tomato sauce, and spaghetti sauce enough for all of our family and many friends. We are grateful for our many blessings.

SUNDAY — OCTOBER 27

ONE of the Pharisees tested Him with this question, "Master, which is the greatest commandment in the Law?"

Jesus answered, "Love the Lord thy God with all your heart, with all your soul, with all your mind. That is the greatest commandment. The second is like unto it. Love your neighbour as yourself. Everything in the law and commandments hang on these two commandments."

— Matthew 22:36-40

MONDAY — OCTOBER 28

GOD has given us memories so that we might always have a good day.

TUESDAY — OCTOBER 29

TRY to keep an open hand. If you go through life with a clenched fist, nobody can ever put anything into it.

WEDNESDAY — OCTOBER 30

PHYLLIS, Bill and the twins came over this evening to carve pumpkins with their Grandpa, Bruce.

It's really interesting to see the changes in the children from year to year. Last year the children were interested only in the carving outcome — the jack-o-lantern's face. This year there were many more questions:

"Grandpa, what is this stringy stuff inside?"

"How many seeds do you think there are?"

"How do you make pumpkin pie?"

"If I plant this seed will a pumpkin grow?"

It seems such as short time ago that they were in highchairs, fascinated by the candlelight of the jack-o-lantern, and now they want to know everything about pumpkins.

Time surely flies.

THURSDAY — OCTOBER 31

FROM ghoulies and ghosties and long-leggety beasties
And things that go bump in the night,
Good Lord, deliver us!

— *Scottish prayer*

November

THAN these November skies
Is no sky lovelier. The clouds are deep;
Into their grey the subtle spies
Of colour creep,
Changing that high austerity to delight,
Till ev'n the leaden interfolds are bright.
And, where the cloud breaks, faint far azure
   peers
Ere a thin flushing cloud again
Shuts out that loveliness, or shares.
The huge great clouds move slowly, gently, as
Reluctant the quick sun should shine in vain,
Holding in bright caprice their rain.
And when of colours none,
Nor rose, nor amber, nor the scarce late green
Is truly seen —
In all the myriad grey,
In silver height and dusky deep, remain
The loveliest,
Faint purple flushes of the unvanquished sun.
— *John Freeman*

THE HERITAGE BOOK

TODAY I had a chance to visit an elderly friend who is living in a nearby nursing home. Martha hadn't been too well lately and so it was with surprise that I found her in the recreation room of the home, playing cards. She was immaculately dressed, her hair was newly permed and she looked wonderfully happy and healthy.

When I expressed my delight at this seemingly drastic change, her reply delighted me.

"Edna, I am eighty-seven years old and for some time I was feeling every minute of my age. But last week, on my birthday, my great-granddaughter Jodie came to wish me a happy birthday. Her gift to me was a subscription to my favourite magazine. But Edna, the subscription was for ten years! Somehow, I decided, I would like to justify that darling girl's faith in my longevity. So I decided that if I'm going to be around for another ten years I'd better make the most of each day and enjoy myself. That's why I look and feel so much better!"

Sometimes the faith of children is what restores the faith of an adult.

THE HERITAGE BOOK

GOD loved the world so much that he gave his only son, that everyone who has faith in Him may not die but have eternal life. It was not to judge the world that God sent his son, but that through him the world might be saved.

ON this day in 1879, the great American humourist, Will Rogers, was born in Oolagah, Oklahoma. He began as a vaudeville trick-rope artist, but when he discovered that audiences liked to hear him talk, he went on to be a monologist, lecturer, newspaper columnist, and movie actor. Government and politics became his favourite targets for jokes like this one: "I do not belong to any organized party. I am a democrat."

When he first made this type of remark on radio in the 1930s, people were shocked. But thanks to his good-humoured delivery, the needling of sacred institutions became popular mass entertainment, and people were able to take things a little less seriously. His most recognized saying (and my favourite), is "I never met a man I didn't like."

TUESDAY — NOVEMBER 5

O NE of the secrets of a long and fruitful life is to forgive everybody everything every night before you go to bed.

WEDNESDAY — NOVEMBER 6

I ENJOYED Sir Winston Churchill's comments on religion: "I have always been surprised to see some of our bishops and clergy making such heavy weather about reconciling the Bible story with modern scientific and historical knowledge.

Why do they want to reconcile them? If you are the recipient of a message which cheers your heart and fortifies your soul, which promises you reunion with those you have loved in a world of larger opportunities and wider sympathies, why should you worry about the shape or colour of the travel-stained envelope; whether it is duly stamped, whether the date on the postmark is right or wrong? These matters may be puzzling, but they are certainly not important. What is important is the message and the benefits to you of receiving it."

THE HERITAGE BOOK

O UR life is like some vast lake that is slowly filling with the stream of our years. As the waters creep surely upward, the landmarks of the past are one by one submerged. But there shall always be memory to lift its head above the tide until the lake is overflowing.

— Alexander Bisson

J UST over two years ago the Berlin Wall, the concrete and barbed-wire horror that separated East and West Berlin, was broken down. From 1961 to 1989 the wall had prevented the East German people from crossing to the west. Families had been separated; many were shot trying to escape from east to west.

One of the many interesting stories to come out at the time of the Wall's opening was that of an East Berlin man. A student in 1961, he had borrowed a book from the West Berlin library, and, after the border closing, had never returned the book. When the wall opened in 1989, his library fine for the overdue book was in excess of $3,000.00. The library forgave the fine.

MY son-in-law John has been dieting in recent weeks. When one of his parishoners asked about his self-denial at the deacon's dinner meeting, he explained it this way, "I'm a calorie-fighter, and recently I've spent too much time fraternizing with the enemy."

ONE of my favourite hymns for this Remembrance Day Sunday is "Onward Christian Soldiers."

Onward Christian soldiers,
Marching as to war,
With the Cross of Jesus
Going on before.
Christ the royal Master,
Leads against the foe,
Forward into battle,
See his banners go.
Onward Christian soldier,
Marching as to war
With the Cross of Jesus
Going on before.

— *Rev. S. Baring-Gould*

MONDAY — NOVEMBER 11
Remembrance Day

THE young people of today have no remembrance of war and of that I am grateful. For who among us wants to think of a brother, or father, or son saying good-bye, never to return home?

Who wants to remember lying in cold trenches in ankle-deep water, hearing the whine of bullets as they pass just overhead? Who wants to see the minister as he gets out of his car and heads up the walkway, trying somehow to find words of comfort for a young mother made suddenly a widow. It is enough that some of us have to bear those memories. Let us fervently hope that we never need do so again. Let peace be in our prayers; let peace in all the world come in our time.

TUESDAY — NOVEMBER 12

AN elderly lady in our church group once told us her wonderful philosophy of life.

"I try to love so that somebody will miss me when I'm gone."

THE HERITAGE BOOK

PEOPLE often warn us against letting the golden hours slip by; but some of them are golden only because we let them slip by.

LIFE is short and we never have enough time for gladdening the hearts of those who travel the way with us. Oh, be swift to love! Make haste to be kind!

— *Henri Frédéric Amiel*

A HUNDRED times every day I remind myself that my inner and outer life depend on the labours of other men, living and dead, and that I must exert myself in order to give in the same measure as I have received and am still receiving.

— *Albert Einstein*

THE HERITAGE BOOK

MY friend Jake and I enjoyed this afternoon's presentation of the show-jumping competition from the Royal Winter Fair. Watching today's exhibition reminded Jake of an interesting equestrian story from the 1960 Olympic Games in Rome.

James William Roycroft was a member of the Australian Olympic Equestrian team competing in the 3-day event.

Day one saw the Australians in fifth place. Day two saw twelve nations eliminated as horses refused fences or fell. Bill Roycroft and his horse "Our Solo" approached a difficult jump. The horse broke the top rail, turned turtle and landed on Roycroft. Regaining consciousness, Bill knew he had to get on the horse or be disqualified. He got on, cleared the last four jumps, and then went by ambulance to the hospital. His injuries included a broken bone in his shoulder, a dislocated collarbone, a severe concussion, and abrasions.

Despite his injuries, he checked himself out of the hospital and returned for the final competition. Though the searing pain threatened to render him unconscious, he completed a perfect round. Roycroft and the Australian team won the gold medal. It was a tribute to one man's courage.

SUNDAY — NOVEMBER 17

THE days of our years are threescore years and ten; and if by reason of strength they be fourscore years, yet is their strength labour and sorrow; for it is soon cut off, and we fly away.

— *Psalm 90:10*

MONDAY — NOVEMBER 18

I PASS judgement not on those who live under a dictatorship and cannot speak but on those who live in freedom and fail to do so.

— *Manés Sperber*

TUESDAY — NOVEMBER 19

LIFE'S heaviest burden is to have nothing to carry.

WEDNESDAY — NOVEMBER 20

THE only ideas that will work for you are the ones that you put to work.

THURSDAY — NOVEMBER 21

A GREAT man is he who has not lost the heart of a child.

— *Mencius*

FRIDAY — NOVEMBER 22

L ET us begin anew — remembering on both sides that civility is not a sign of weakness, and sincerity is always subject to proof. Let us never negotiate out of fear. But let us never fear to negotiate.

— *John F. Kennedy*

SATURDAY — NOVEMBER 23

A WISE old owl sat on an oak,
The more he saw the less he spoke;
The less he spoke the more he heard;
Why aren't we like that wise old bird?

Sunday — November 24

Jesus said to him "I am the way, and the truth, and the life; no one comes to the Father, but through me."

Monday — November 25

I must admit that I find November to be a drab month. There is little to recommend it — the leaves are gone, there is no snow to whiten the landscape, the sky is often grey.

Several readers have offered their suggestions as to how to add some cheer:

One lady suggests wearing only brightly-coloured clothing, "This at least makes me feel cheerier."

Another gentleman suggests planning several get-togethers with close friends. "Time spent in good company always seems brighter."

Yet another reader has the quintessential answer — spend November in Florida.

Tuesday — November 26

An apology is a good way to have the last word.

THE HERITAGE BOOK

I LOVE my humble fireside
Where I can sit and dream.

I see strange pictures in the flames
And memories bring tears;
I live again the yesterdays
And joys of other years.

And then I hear loved voices low,
So happy, cheerful and gay
These dreams remain so dear to me
When the firelight dies away.

I love my humble fireside
Where I can sit and dream.

— Grace M. Walker

PERHAPS the most valuable result of all education is the ability to make yourself do the
thing you have to do, when it ought to be
done, whether you like it or not; it is the first
lesson that ought to be learned; and however
early a man's training begins, it is probably the
last lesson that he learns thoroughly.

— Thomas Henry Huxley

WE have new neighbours on our block — a young couple with two small children.

Marg made a casserole for them on moving day and was surprised when the young mother called her by name.

"Oh, I knew you must be Marg," she said. "Mrs. Watson left wonderful notes for us. She described the neighbours, told us a little about each family and then left us the names of a doctor, a dentist, the best restaurants to take small children to and lots of other interesting things to see and do in this area. I know we're going to love it here!"

What a lovely way to welcome a new family.

SATURDAY — NOVEMBER 30

WHENEVER a man's friends begin to compliment him about looking young, he may be sure that they think he is growing old.

— *Washington Irving*

December

SUNDAY — DECEMBER 1

O COME, O come, Emmanuel
And ransome captive Israel,
That mourns in lowly exile here,
Until the son of God appear.
Rejoice! rejoice! Emmanuel
Shall come to thee, O Israel.

MONDAY — DECEMBER 2

DECEMBER has arrived and with it came a beautiful white blanket of snow. The snow, though it heralds the beginning of a long winter, was a beautiful sight after the grey-brown shades of November. As it sparkled in the morning sun, it brightened and cheered me and gave me a big lift for the day. Isn't it silly how a little bit of snow can be so uplifting?

THE HERITAGE BOOK

THE snow began in the evening,
Scattered by an unseen hand,
Transforming familiar landmarks
Into a winter wonderland.

The sun shone bright with morning,
The sky was of deepest blue,
The snow was enchanting with fairies dancing.
And it sparkled all the day through.

— *author unknown*

WEDNESDAY — DECEMBER 4

THE story is that on the night of December 4, 1877, some of the people in Thomas Edison's laboratory at Menlo Park, New Jersey sat up all night playing with a newly-completed device — the phonograph. From that primitive beginning has evolved such an amazing array of recording instruments that the phonograph and records are all but obsolete. Wouldn't Mr. Edison be gratified to hear the amazing quality of compact discs and to know that he was the beginning of it all?

THURSDAY — DECEMBER 5

A LITTLE experience can help a person overcome quite a bit of education.

FRIDAY — DECEMBER 6

MAYBE we should do something that we think we can do well, even if we don't get praise. Birds sing without applause.

SATURDAY — DECEMBER 7

WE never fully comprehend death until it takes someone we love.

SUNDAY — DECEMBER 8

NOW the God of hope fill you with all joy and peace in believing that ye may abound in hope, through the power of the Holy Ghost.

— Book of Common Prayer

THE HERITAGE BOOK

THIS is such a busy time of year that often our friends and relatives in hospitals or nursing homes don't receive as much company as they might usually.

With this in mind I decided to visit May Parker, an elderly friend of mine who resides in the chronic care unit of our hospital. May was in the lounge with a number of the other residents, enjoying a concert of Christmas carols with several of the nurses and interns.

As they sang, a group of about twenty very young children came into the room. They were a class of Grade 1 students on a tour of the hospital. Fred, the organist, asked one of the youngsters if their group would sing a song and the child immediately replied, "Sure — can you play Jingle Bells?"

Fred struck up a sparkling rendition of that old favourite and the children sang, their clear sweet voices showing the wonderful enthusiasm of their youth. Gradually the others joined in, many with quavering voices and others with tears in their eyes.

It was truly a beautiful experience.

THE HERITAGE BOOK

MARG and I finally finished our Christmas cards today. Each year I seem to be just a little slower getting them addressed and ready to go. Perhaps it's because I write a letter to accompany each card, and every year I seem to have more news about my growing family. (I certainly wouldn't like to think that my advancing age has anything to do with it!)

Whatever the reason, I can only hope our post office will make up for my shortcomings and deliver my cards before Christmas Day arrives.

WE pity in others only those evils which we ourselves have experienced.
— *Jean Jacques Rousseau*

AMBITION never gets anywhere until it forms a partnership with work.

FRIDAY — DECEMBER 13

L IGHT looked down and beheld Darkness
  "Thither will I go," said Light.
Peace looked down and beheld War
"Thither will I go," said Peace.
Love looked down and beheld Hatred
"Thither will I go," said Love.
So came Light and shone;
So came Peace and gave rest;
So came Love and brought life
And the word was made flesh
And dwelt among us.

— Laurence Housman

SATURDAY — DECEMBER 14

I WATCHED the children sledding on the hill in
  our park today. One youngster, shouting
happily, was on his brand new brightly col-
oured plastic coaster. His friend, equally
happy, was sliding on the cardboard box that
the sled came in.

THE HERITAGE BOOK

A<small>ND</small> the angel said to her, "Do not be afraid, Mary, for you have found favour with God. And behold, you will conceive in your womb, and bear a son, and you shall name him Jesus."

— *Luke 1: 30-31*

I<small>N</small> winters past, the sounds of jingle bells and laughter often filled the frosty air. On snowy evenings, families would climb into their horse-drawn sleighs and enjoy a ride.

In most areas these sleighs are gone, leaving just a few oldsters with pleasant memories. However many of the "Pioneer Villages" still offer rides in the old-time horse-drawn sleighs and it can be a joyous family outing to enjoy the pleasure of this long ago winter pastime. Perhaps you could make it a Christmas gift for grandchildren, or great-grandchildren. It's certainly something they wouldn't soon forget.

Tuesday — December 17

Marshall and his wife Jamie stopped by this evening. Jamie is visibly pregnant now and bubbling enthusiastically about her pending motherhood. She showed me a card that friends had given her with this inscription:

"A baby will make love stronger, days shorter, nights longer, bankroll smaller, home happier, clothes shabbier, the past forgotten, and the future worth living for."

Wednesday — December 18

Have you had a kindness shown?
Pass it on.

— Henry Burton

Thursday — December 19

One of the nicest things about this time of year is that people seem to make an extra effort to contact old friends. This evening a very dear friend of ours from Pennsylvania arrived for dinner. It had been a number of years since we'd seen Don, but we fell into conversation as if it had been merely days. Perhaps this is the greatest joy of old friendships.

THE HERITAGE BOOK

ERMA Bombeck's humour appeals to me very much. She writes, "Cold weather, especially snow, tends to limit children's activities. They can't go to school in it, take out the garbage in it, go to the dentist in it, or shovel the driveway in it. They can, however, ski in it, sled in it, ice skate in it, roll in it and eat it."

THE Christmas log — it's a hearth-warming sight.

HEAVENLY Father; who chose the Virgin Mary, full of grace, to be the mother of our Lord and Saviour, now fill us with your grace, that we, in all things, may embrace your will and with her, rejoice in your salvation through Jesus Christ our Lord. Amen.

— *Book of Common Prayer*

THE HERITAGE BOOK

THERE seems to be an endless number of last-minute things to do before Wednesday. Many of the things have to do with the family's Christmas dinner, which is being held here at Marg and Bruce's home. Even though these few days are hectic, I try to find a quiet time to seek peace and to rejoice in the reason that we celebrate the glorious day of Christ's birth. I hope that all of you may find time to thank God for the precious gift of his son.

AT this evening's carol service we sang one of my very favourite carols — "Good Christian Men Rejoice."

Good Christian men, rejoice
With heart and soul and voice,
Give ye heed to what we say:
News! News!
Jesus Christ is born today!
Ox and ass before Him bow
And he is in the manger now.
Christ is born today!
Christ is born today!

THE HERITAGE BOOK

O GOD, who makest us glad with the yearly remembrance of the birth of thy only Son, Jesus Christ: Grant that as we joyfully receive him as our Redeemer we may with sure confidence behold him when he shall come again to be our Judge: who liveth and reigneth with thee and the Holy Ghost now and ever.

Amen.

— Book of Common Prayer,
Christmas collect

THURSDAY — DECEMBER 26

J OSEPH Haydn, on being criticized for the gaiety of his church music, responded, "I cannot help it. I give forth what is in me. When I think of the Divine Being, my heart is so full of joy that the notes fly off as from a spindle. And as I have a cheerful heart, He will pardon me if I serve Him cheerfully."

FRIDAY — DECEMBER 27

A s gold more splendid from the fire appears, thus friendship brightens by the length of years.

— Thomas Carlyle

THE HERITAGE BOOK

B UT beauty seen is never lost,
God's colours all are fast;
The glory of this sunset heaven
Into my soul has passed.

— *John Greenleaf Whittier*

F ATHER, we pray thee for the vision which
sees
Beyond the things of time and sense.
Beyond the vain attractions of this world,
Where we abide for but a few days,
To the eternal realities —
To the deathless truth and beauty of love
For whose sake Thou hast given us being.

— *John S. Hoyland*

MONDAY — DECEMBER 30

O F all earthly music, that which reaches the farthest into heaven is the beating of a loving heart.

— Henry Ward Beecher

TUESDAY — DECEMBER 31

A s the year draws to a close, may I wish for all of you a happy and healthy New Year. God bless you all!